The Recipe Book

Practical ideas for the language classroom

Pilgrims

Edited by Seth Lindstromberg

Longman

Longman Group UK Limited,
Longman House, Burnt Mill, Harlow,
Essex CM20 2JE, England
and Associated Companies throughout the world.

© Longman Group UK Limited 1990

This book is produced in association
with Pilgrims Language Courses Limited
of Canterbury, England.

First published 1990
Second impression 1990

Set in Linotron 10/12pt Cheltenham

Printed in Great Britain
by Richard Clay plc, Bungay, Suffolk

British Library Cataloguing in Publication Data
Lindstromberg, Seth
    The *Recipe Book* : practical ideas for the language
    classroom. – (Pilgrims Longman teachers resource book)
    1. Schools. Curriculum subjects. English language.
    Teaching
    I. Title
    420.71

ISBN 0 582 037646

Acknowledgements
We are grateful to the following for permission to reproduce
copyright material:
Jonathan Cape Ltd on behalf of the Estate of Robert
Frost/Henry Holt Inc for poem 'Mending Wall' from *The
Poetry of Robert Frost* edited by Edward Connery Latham,
US Copyright (c) 1969 by Holt Rinehart & Winston Inc.
Copyright (c) 1962 by Robert Frost. Copyright (c) 1975 by
Lesley Frost Ballantine; Ewan Macnaughton Associates as
Syndication Agents for *The Daily Telegraph* for extract
from article in *The Daily Telegraph* 21.1.87; Guardian News
Service Ltd for news item 'Cat's Feat' in *The Guardian*
9.6.87; IPC Magazines Ltd for article 'Decimals flummox
maths pupils' in *New Scientist* 10.7.86; Pitman Publishing
for an extract from *Teaching as a Subversive Activity* by
N. Postman & C. Weingartner.
We have unfortunately been unable to trace the copyright
holders of the news items in *The Daily Telegraph* 21.1.87,
The Times 27.5.87. and would appreciate any information
which would enable us to do so.

We are grateful to the following for permission to
reproduce copyright illustrative material:
The Independent for the Weather Forecast on page 72 in
The Independent 22.7.89: London Transport Museum for
the advertisement on page 57.

Illustrations
Cover illustrated by Ian Whadcock

A letter from the Series Editors

Dear Teacher,

This series of teachers' resource books has developed from Pilgrims' involvement in running courses for learners of English and for teachers and teacher trainers.

Our aim is to pass on ideas, techniques and practical activities which we know work in the classroom. Our authors, both Pilgrims teachers and like-minded colleagues in other organisations, present accounts of innovative procedures which will broaden the range of options available to teachers working within communicative and humanistic approaches.

We would be very interested to receive your impressions of the series. If you notice any omissions that we ought to rectify in future editions, or if you think of any interesting variations, please let us know. We will be glad to acknowledge all contributions that we are able to use.

Seth Lindstromberg
Series Editor

Mario Rinvolucri
Series Consultant

Pilgrims Language Courses
Canterbury
Kent
CT1 3HG
England

Seth Lindstromberg

Seth Lindstromberg spent his early childhood in small town Oregon and his teens in rural Illinois. In 1969, after four years at the University of Washington and spells of farm, janitorial, kitchen, cannery and longshore work, he was awarded a BA in Eastern European History and, a year later, an MA in History from the University of Toronto. Next came several years of taxi driving, construction and sawmill work, and, eventually, a year of teacher training at Simon Fraser University in British Columbia. Since 1978 he has taught EFL in Japan, Switzerland and England. He first taught for Pilgrims in 1985. He recently received an M Phil in Applied Linguistics (Lexicography) from the University of Exeter and is a frequent contributor of articles, mainly on word teaching, to a variety of ELT publications. Seth and his wife Tessa Woodward teach at Hilderstone College, Kent.

Contents

Index of activities

Introduction

Who is this book for?

This book is for teachers who want to teach interesting lessons for the sake of better learning. More particularly, it's for teachers who already have some experience with communicative language teaching but who find that the communicative materials of the day lack the vividness of life. It's for teachers who want their learners, sometimes at least, to *use* the target language in the classroom, not just *imitate* use.

The Recipe Book is for teachers of any foreign or second language. Although written with English in mind, only one of the activities in it (*The Earth and Whizbango*) could be difficult to apply in teaching a different language.

Teachers in most situations will find the book useful. The activities it presents have grown out of the experience of teachers who have, collectively, worked in a great variety of situations all over the world. There are, for example, ideas here that will work with classes of fifty Japanese college students (e.g. Jean-Paul Creton's *Do it Yourself Story*), and others you can use with middle-aged business people, one-to-one (e.g. Mario Rinvolucri's *Personalised Listening Comprehension*). Many of the activities suit both of these example teaching situations and most others besides (e.g. Jane and Dave Willis's *Unpacking Sentences*).

There are ideas here for teachers in well-resourced schools as well as for ones with a group of learners, and just the sky above and the earth below (e.g. John Morgan's role plays).

Learners of all levels of proficiency are catered for, even the truly advanced ... and activities which challenge people at this level are extremely useful.

Is there a limitation in appeal?

This book is primarily for people who teach older teens and upwards rather than children. Still, some of the warm-ups, for example, will work at least as well with children as with adults. Judy Baker's *Verbal Dynamics* is perfect for children.

What's in the book?

Among the activities are warm-ups and complete lessons that learners can really get their teeth into.

There are rigorous vocabulary learning lessons with the aim of equipping learners with strategies and techniques of general use in word learning.

There are activities, too, which focus on accuracy in pronunciation and grammar. The four skills are amply catered for.

How can this book fit into a course?

Most teachers will use this collection as a source of supplementary activities. It could serve, though, as a principal source of inspiration for a two-week to one-month intensive course for learners who have had enough of traditional teaching and yearn for a chance to use English in a way that improves their fluency, enlarges their vocabulary, and is generally more interesting.

Background and rationale

This book, like its predecessor *Recipes for Tired Teachers* (Sion 1985), began, for the most part, in the staffroom of the Pilgrims Summer School at the University of Kent, Canterbury, England. Since the mid-1970s it has been the custom of Pilgrims teachers to share novel activities by pinning them up on the 'recipe board' for use, adaptation, and comment. The activities here, with a few exceptions, come from the four summers of 1985 to 1988.

Though diverse, the collection is representative of a particular view of language learning and teaching: people learn a language better if their experience in it is as full of meaning and as rich in images as possible. Meaning and mental images come only when connection is made with learners' own world of experience. The greater the connection, the better the learning. Hence the emphasis placed in this collection is on drawing on the experience of learners (and teachers) themselves, rather than on the concerns of invented characters in this or that story line of a textbook.

Most classroom language learning activities are seriously lacking in this area. Take, for example, a role play in which learners are expected to imagine they are in no particular train station speaking about departure times for imaginary trains going to arbitrary destinations. This is real and meaningful language use only in the sense that a picture of a flower is a flower. John Morgan's role plays are light years away from such pale situational work. But there are dozens of other real, not merely realistic, conversational activities here too. One of the first I tried out myself is Peter Grundy's gem, *Habits*.

Of course, most learners also want language analysis and practice. Accordingly, there is a section of ideas for accuracy work. However, it is conversational activities that predominate in *The Recipe Book* for the reason that there already exist mountains of materials devoted to analysis and controlled practice of the grammatical details of English.

The 'Recipe'

A language teacher who is native or near-native in their teaching tongue knows some tens of thousands of its words, is aware of the ins and outs of usage, possesses an immense capacity to generate language spontaneously, and has years of life experience. Such a teacher has infinitely more potential to adapt to the needs of their learners and the flux of the classroom than any textbook. This does not mean that teachers should suddenly never use textbooks again. There is no doubt, though, that many teachers use textbooks far too much and far too inflexibly, and require some liberation from their thrall. We believe that there are ideas in this book that will start a great many of its readers off on the road to making what they do in class – even textbook work – more interesting by encouraging them to draw more on their own huge mental resources.

In this connection, Mario Rinvolucri has spoken of the power of the 'recipe' to function as a benign Trojan Horse in the development of a teacher. His line of thought goes something like this:

If a teacher uses an activity involving an unfamiliar technique, they may incorporate this technique into their repertoire if it works well. They may use it in other activities too. If the technique is an expression of an approach (or a method) unfamiliar to the teacher, pennies may begin to drop and the teacher may take on a practical competence in the new approach 'from the bottom up'.

Accordingly, we need not agree with the all too common, though 'expert' opinion that worthwhile sophistication of thought necessarily begins with theory and high level methodology and works its way down to practice. One result of the prevalence of this view in what some chose to term 'teacher education' is a poverty in technique for those who come into teaching by this route. But let's get back to the idea that activities are things that can have techniques in them.

Tessa Woodward has noted in her article Splitting the Atom (*English Teaching Forum* 1988) that language teaching activities are composed of independent elements that can be combined in different, even surprising ways. She groups these elements in eleven major categories. Here are the first three:

1 Organisation (How are the people and furniture arranged?)
2 Materials/aids, e.g.:
   The writing surface: on the board, on a poster, on an OHP transparency, in learners' notebooks, on little slips of paper, on potatoes (seriously!), on people, . . .
3 Process (What do the various participants do?), e.g.:
   Who writes? The teacher, one learner, everyone . . .
   Who reads? No one, an unspecified imaginary person, a real but absent person, the teacher, one learner, everyone, . . .

Her message is that if teachers are aware of a wide range of options in the choice and combination of elements, then they have an immensely powerful tool not only for adapting activities to fit different situations, but also for creating, in effect, wholly new activities. All that is necessary is a willingness to consider seemingly odd combinations like, 'Everyone is seated, including the teacher (who is not in a 'leading' position) and everyone in the class writes to everyone else in the class on little slips of paper'. Now look at the sequence of letter writing activities by Mario Rinvolucri and Cynthia Beresford (Chapter Eight).

A word on organisation

The fact that activities are complex has an inescapable implication for the organisation of a book like this. Ordering and chaptering are always imperfect. Accordingly, traditional criteria seem as good as any here. For example, Chapter One, Warm-ups, breaks and fillers, comprises activities that tend to be short and good for particular phases within a longer lesson; the activities in Chapter Eight, Especially Writing, share a particular skill focus; those in Chapter Seven, Story Telling, all involve creation of the same general kind of text.

The presentation of the activities

We have adopted numbered step-by-step description of the activities and address the teacher-reader as 'you'. All in all, the style is informal. *They*, *their*, etc. are allowed to have their conversationally natural potential for both singular and plural reference (not unlike the word *you*).

Level and time are given for each activity. The latter is, of course, highly variable, especially with regard to the longer activities.

The skills the learners will be applying are specified, as appropriate. Under the 'skills focus' heading we mean to highlight any involvement of individual skills that goes beyond such routine activity as the learners listening to the teacher's instructions or their writing the odd note in their notebooks. Often, the skills are listed in the order in which they come up in the activity at hand. Where this order is impossible to specify, the usual order of 'listening, speaking, reading, writing' is followed.

Also specified, under the heading 'extras', are materials and aids you will need over and above such things as pens and paper and a decent board to write on.

The language focus is specified where there happens to be one.

The rationale is given when it's slightly unusual.

In many cases, contributors have listed variations, to start you off in your adaptations.

Acknowledgements

Some of the activities have appeared elsewhere, though not in the same form as here. All of the warm-ups written or contributed by Tessa Woodward have appeared in her column *Warm-ups, Breaks and Fillers* in the *ETAS Newsletter* (English Teachers' Association of Switzerland) from 1984 to 1989. Jean Paul Creton's *Do-it-Yourself Stories* has appeared in his book *Day by Day* (1983, p. 21).

Six of the activities appear, in outline, in *Storytelling im Englischunter-richt* (Wicke 1988) in an appendix of ideas from Pilgrims teachers. They are: Jim Wingate's *Greetings*, *Circle Step*, and *Behind a Song*; Cynthia Beresford's *Sound Sequence* and *Stories from Things*; and Judy Baker's *Seven Stages Story Telling*. I would like to thank Chris Edelhoff of the Hessische Institut für Lehrfortbildung for kindly providing me with a copy of Rainer Wicke's book and for agreeing to our use of these activities.

Exercises around numbers role play, *Photo Proxies*, *Invisible Pictures*, *The Empty Chair 1 & 2*, and *Doubling 1 & 2*, derive from an essay by John Morgan first published by CPLE Roubaix in their house magazine *Bazar* (2:3 1 Fevrier 1986), and appear in *The Recipe Book* by kind permission of the Editor, Lynn Delmotte.

I would also like to thank:

- Pilgrims for providing typing in the early stages of putting this book together and for providing the means to type in the later stages
- Tessa Woodward, especially for her work on Chapter One and for comments on the introduction
- John Morgan for most of Chapters Three and Four
- Mario Rinvolucri and Marion Cooper for their astute and helpful comments throughout
- Jim Wingate for compiling an earlier collection of activities

Finally . . .

It is unlikely that there can now be a language teaching activity new in all of its elements. But considered as wholes, most of the activities in this book are, we think, quite new. One or two are based on fairly well-known activities but have been varied or extended in a useful way. There are a few activities, such as Tessa Woodward's *Points of Contact*, which are known in another branch of teaching (drama, in this case) but which are not well-known among language teachers.

Where an activity has been borrowed or adapted, from within language teaching or without, we have tried always to acknowledge its source. Memory sometimes fails though. If you come across an activity which you feel ought to be acknowledged but isn't or which ought to be acknowledged differently than it is, please do let us know.

Seth Lindstromberg
Pilgrims
Canterbury 1989.

CHAPTER 1

Warm-ups, breaks and fillers

When I first went to work at the International Language Centre in Kanda, Tokyo, in the late 1970s, there was an in-house style that favoured the use of 'warm-ups', 'breaks', and 'fillers'. I picked up the habit and it's been with me ever since. And I expect I've passed it on to quite a few colleagues by now too.

Let's look at the rationale of using short activities at different stages of a lesson, activities which may not necessarily have a clear and direct connection with anything else. To start with, in Fig. 1 you can see how concentration on the (teacher's!) topic of a lesson grows and flags over the course of a lesson (in longer lessons the curve stays low):

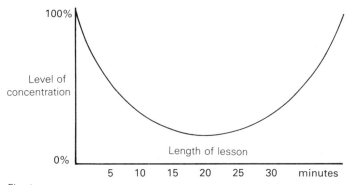

Fig. 1

Naturally, teachers will want to know why the curve has such low segments, and if or how they can be raised.

When people first come into class they may feel cold, hot, tired, eager to see each other, or full of some recent experience. The chances are strong that they will not immediately give 100 per cent concentration to the lesson and will not pull together all at once as a group. The idea of a warm-up exercise, then, is to ease everybody into the lesson in an interesting, informal, and enjoyable way.

People have different concentration spans. Some can absorb themselves in an interesting task for hours. Others are butterflies and need to keep moving from activity to activity in order to stay interested. Most people seem to have natural attention-wandering phases several times a lesson. Break activities accept this fact and embrace it by deliberately giving people a chance to do something different ... whether it is to stand up, sit down, move around, look out of the window, shut their eyes, listen to music, listen to the trees, or to do a short, interestingly different break activity.

It's possible that towards the end of a lesson, people start to get tired, or to think about transport or about what they are going to do when the class ends. Alternatively, there are times when learners work through exercises faster than the teacher expects or when the teacher has prepared too little material. This can be a nerve-wracking experience for a novice teacher who feels guilty about letting learners go early or about just chatting. It can lead experienced teachers, too, into the pitfalls of asking learners to swap parts 'just one more time' in a role play that is past its prime. To combat these problems, teachers can carry around with them a list of fillers that can help the last part of a lesson go with a swing rather than just fizzling out.

By building up a repertoire of activities that can be used as warm-ups, breaks or fillers, by observing learners carefully to see the signs of fatigue, boredom, or inactivity, the curve in our first graph can be transformed to look something like the one in Fig. 2. (For more information on learning with and without breaks see *Use Your Head*, Buzan 1982.) Well-designed

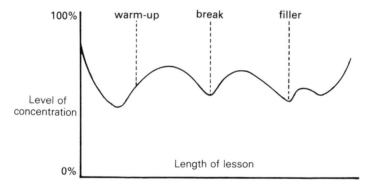

Fig. 2

short activities can be easily broken off (e.g. when the bell goes) or added to at any time (e.g. for early-comers with a little time on their hands), initiated by learners (they can do one they've done before and start it before you arrive!). The activities can focus on a learning point (such as vocabulary) that is always there to fall back on and which is a safety net for the teacher new to the business of timing phases of a lesson to suit institutional lesson times.

Warm-ups, breaks, and fillers can be chosen to harmonise with the main theme of the lesson or to achieve a smooth rounding off of one phase and a gentle transition to the next. Thus, for example, *Blackboard Feelings* can ease you into a translation lesson. *Head, Shoulders, Knees, and Toes* can round off a lesson on the vocabulary of the parts of the body. To move from a listening comprehension to an unrelated writing exercise, you can put the words *interlude* or *writing exercise* on the board and ask learners to make as many new words as they can from them. (Start them off with a couple of examples.) The exercise can take just two minutes.

The basic idea here is to build a collection of short activities you can use to increase concentration, change pace, brighten up, raise energy, or calm down ... in short, so that you can weave more variety into your lessons for the benefit of your learners ... and you too. Have fun!

Tessa Woodward

BLACKBOARD FEELINGS

If a learner can only manage to come to a language class once or twice a week, it can be very hard to go from speaking the mother tongue at home, at work, in the street, and in the shops, to a sudden requirement to speak English, all English and nothing but English in the language classroom. Here are a couple of ideas for gently leaving the mother tongue and moving into English. Ideas that mean too that the teacher has to start from where the learners are and how they are feeling.

Procedure

1 At the start of the lesson, encourage your learners to come to the board and write in their mother tongue a few words that express how they feel, what sort of day/week/weekend they've had or something else they want to say. Thus someone might write, *Que je suis fatiguée!* or *Gruetzi mitenand!* After a few minutes you should have quite a few utterances on the board.

2 The next step is to ask people, if they can, to silently write an English translation above any of the phrases that have been written up on the board.

3 Someone might come up and write *I'm tired* above *Que je suis fatiguée!* If the person who wrote the original phrase doesn't feel the translation is quite right, they simply shake their head. Both phrases stay on the board. Someone else may come up and write *Hello everybody!* above the *Gruetzi Mitenand* message. If the translation is accepted, the writer of the original phrase nods his/her head and the teacher wipes out the Swiss-German phrase. Someone may eventually come up with something like *Oh boy am I tired!* for *Que je suis fatiguée!* and if this is accepted, then the French phrase goes. By the end of the exercise most of the phrases on the board will be in English.

4 People can now choose any of these phrases and say them to anyone else in the room. English has started, learners are saying what they feel and the teacher knows how they feel.

1.1

LEVEL
Beginner +

EXTRAS
None

TIME
10 minutes

SKILLS FOCUS
All four, but with short utterances

Tessa Woodward

1.2

LEVEL
Post-beginner

EXTRAS
None

TIME
10 minutes

SKILLS FOCUS
Speaking and
listening

Tessa Woodward

MILLING PHRASES

Procedure

1 For this exercise, push the chairs back and let people mill around the room. First they mill silently. When they pass someone, they simply glance at them and glance away again.

2 After a minute or two of this, you then say that when they pass someone they say one, two or three words to the person in English. Greeting words and phrases such as *Hello!* or *Good evening!* are not allowed. People can say words that they like (e.g. *serene* or *pearl* or *thingummyjig*) or words they've just learnt or any word they can remember.

3 People mill around saying the odd word or two and listening to other people's words. If they hear something they like they can take it over and repeat it themselves. After a minute or two they can build up phrases of a maximum of six words.

4 Then, ask everyone to stop. As a whole class, people comment on any funny or intriguing words or phrases that came up. People can ask any question they like to a fellow learner (e.g. *What's a thingummy ...?*, *Why did you choose that word?*) or to the teacher. Again the sounds have gradually become English and the input is the learners' own.

VARIATIONS

Just as you can 'cannibalise' one car by removing its engine in order to place it in the good chassis of another car, so you can switch the parts of the two exercises above. *Blackboard Feelings* can be changed so that people scatter up on the board the odd few words that they like or remember. *Milling phrases* can start off in the mother tongue and people can find translations for each other as they pass by. Or maybe as you try out either the originals or the variations, new variations will come to you. You can adapt them anyway you like to make them fit your style and your needs.

RIGHT WORD, WRONG WORD

I recently read a marvellous book about improvisation (*Impro* Johnstone 1981) and got an idea for a warm-up from it.

Procedure

1 Ask learners to walk around the room looking at things. When they see something they know the name of in English, they say the name out loud. So learners go around muttering *table ... carpet ... friend ... shirt ... view*, etc. This is a simple review of known vocabulary items.

2 Next ask learners to do the same thing except that they 'share' their word. When they see something they know the name of, they touch another learner on the arm, point to the thing to be named and name it out loud. The person listening then returns the favour by pointing to something else and naming it out loud too. This way vocabulary that one learner knows can be transferred to another.

3 Now for the hilarious part! From now on, learners go around the room spotting things, tapping each other on the arm, pointing to the object to be named and calling out the WRONG name for it! Thus one learner will point at the carpet and shout out, *Ceiling!* Their partner will point to their own nose and say, *Ear*, and so on. At this point laughter will break out, voices will get louder and naming will get more and more outrageous. Soon pairs of learners will come up to the teacher, point and say things like, *Alligator*, burst into fits of laughter and walk away!

1.3

LEVEL
Beginner +

EXTRAS
None

TIME
5 minutes

LANGUAGE FOCUS
Concrete nouns

SKILLS FOCUS
Speaking and listening

Tessa Woodward

LABEL THE ROOM
Procedure

1 Ask your learners to tear up some note paper into label-sized pieces.

2 Tell them that they are going to have five minutes to rush around the room naming all the objects in it but that they are going to do this in a special way.

3 Tell them that they are going to stick labels on things in the room that they know the words for. It works like this – they write the name of an object on one of their labels along with their own name. They stick this label on an object it names so that everyone can read it. That is, someone might stick a label saying 'blackboard — Regula' on the blackboard or a label saying 'wristwatch — Werner' on someone's wristwatch.

If the room is 'yours', you can have the learners use sticky labels or attach the labels with blu-tac or sellotape. Or learners can simply rest their labels on or tuck them under things.

4 When you say *Go!*, the learners rush around writing and placing labels. After five minutes you shout *Stop!*

1.4

LEVEL
Beginner to intermediate

EXTRAS
Sticky labels or slips of paper, blu-tac or sellotape

TIME
10 minutes

LANGUAGE FOCUS
Concrete nouns

SKILLS FOCUS
All four

Tessa Woodward

5 Next you all go around checking the correctness of the labels. 'Clock' attached to a watch is not acceptable. Neither is 'cubboard' on a cupboard. Those who have misspelt something get their label back, correct it and keep it as a tangible reminder of a slight problem which they can solve next time.

The person who has written the most correct labels wins.

FOLLOW ONS AND VARIATIONS

a If you are able to, leave the labels where they are. The next time you need a filler, students can label more things with your help or with the help of bilingual dictionaries. Those who made mistakes last time can write new labels for old problems. Once the objects are named you can move on in later lessons to descriptions. Thus, what was 'desk' becomes a 'rectangular wooden desk' the time after. This can still be competitive if you like, but I find that by this time people usually feel more co-operative asking others to help with phrases like *made of glass*, etc. Leaving the labels may also encourage another class to use them or even add to them, and so foster sharing between classes.

b There's a variation called *Label your neighbour* which is played by writing names of the parts of the body and/or clothing on labels and sticking them all over the person you are sitting next to. This variation can be used in classrooms that don't allow much movement. You might keep an eye on who's sitting next to who for this. But most people seem to find it amusing vocabulary practice!

c A further variation of the original activity is to insist that a correct article be supplied as well. Thus, 'a window sill' if and only if there is more than one window sill and 'the blackboard' if and only if there is just one blackboard. This can be challenging for, say, Oriental students and Slavs, but would obviously not be very interesting for most Western Europeans.

HEAD, SHOULDERS, KNEES AND TOES

1.5

In cold weather, warm-ups need to be taken quite literally in many chilly classrooms! I find that physical exercise with a bit of language practice can help people to thaw out. This activity and the next one are two ideas for warming up elementary level learners.

LEVEL
Elementary

EXTRAS
None

Procedure

TIME
2 minutes if learners know the song, 10 minutes if they don't

1 Start by making sure learners know the vocabulary in the ditty.
2 Show them how to sing it, standing up, to the tune of 'There's a Tavern in the Town' or some other suitable melody.
3 The idea is to touch the part of the body mentioned in the song with the tips of your fingers as you sing it.

SKILLS FOCUS
Speaking and listening

Tessa Woodward

> Head, shoulders, knees and toes,
>   knees and toes.
> Head, shoulders, knees and toes,
>   knees and toes.
> And eyes and ears and mouth and chin,
> Head, shoulders, knees and toes!

4 Once learners have got the hang of it, sing it faster and faster until they're warm. If you don't know the tune, send me a tape (c/o Pilgrims) and I'll sing it for you.

I think this game is played in primary schools as I learned it from a primary school teacher (whose name I have, unfortunately, forgotten).

POINTS OF CONTACT

1.6

Procedure

LEVEL
Beginner +

1 Ask your learners to stand up.
2 You explain that a person standing normally has two points of contact with the floor (i.e. their two feet), four points of contact if their shoes have raised heels. Say/show that if you bend down and put a finger on the floor, you have an additional point of contact (e.g. two feet + one finger = three points of contact).
3 Check your learners' understanding by saying *Five* and watch them make five points of contact with the floor in any way they can. If you have a genteel, well-dressed class, they will manage elegantly and discreetly with hands and fingers. A more comfortably dressed class with a higher energy level will start using foreheads and bottoms and then take shoes and socks off to get a 'toe count'!

EXTRAS
None

TIME
2 to 5 minutes the first time, 1 or 2 minutes thereafter

SKILLS FOCUS
Speaking and listening

Tessa Woodward

4 Now you call out numbers and people have to arrange themselves so that they have that many points of contact with the floor.

VARIATIONS

a Learners call out the numbers to other learners and the teacher.

b People join up into two or three person 'robots' that can achieve, between them, higher numbers. Thus as beginners or elementary learners get better at numbers, a three person robot can be asked to achieve '48'. Of course, all counting between learners, and suggestions like, *Can you put two fingers down?* must be done in English.

The great things about this activity are that it is wonderfully whacky, encourages people to count in English without thinking of it as a chore, and it gets the blood rushing around. Such physical warm-ups are not just useful for thawing out in winter, they can also prevent numb-bottoms all year round!

I learnt this jolly number practice game from my husband, Seth Lindstromberg, who learnt it from Nick Owen, a drama teacher.

1.7

LEVEL
Intermediate +

EXTRAS
None

TIME
5 minutes

SKILLS FOCUS
Speaking and listening

Tessa Woodward

TALKING POINTS

This activity is a quickie for the teacher who's late, out of breath and feeling rushed or who needs to leave early.

Procedure

1 The teacher enters the classroom and says, *OK, somebody choose a letter between A and Z.* Someone obligingly says, for example, *m.*

2 You write that on the board and say, *Right. Give me a noun that starts with m. Marshmallows, Mother, Micky Mouse, Memory,* some learners might say.

3 Right, thanks!, you say, as you write their words on the board.

4 Then you explain, *You have to choose one of those words and talk about the subject any way you can with a partner for three minutes and don't worry about making mistakes. Alright! Start!*

That's it. Learners start buzzing and you have time to put your things down, think, relax and become a teacher and part of the group.

5 Once the learners have been chatting for a while, you can bring them back into a whole group again by ringing a bell, shaking a tambourine or flicking the light switch on and off quickly, all of which are better than shouting.

6 Then you explain to the learners the point of what they've just done. Often in life, in bus queues, in pubs, on the phone, you have to deal

with unexpected subjects when they come up. You can't always pick the subject that YOU want to talk about. You have to adapt fast to other people's topics. So, this warm-up gives practice in dealing with unpredictability. It has, thus, a sound rationale; it's fun; and it needs no preparation. Learners who choose odd letters like *X* or *Z* the first time will learn that they are giving themselves a hard time.

SEQUENCES

If you learn a language in a normal sort of way, unless you go to the country where the language is spoken and stay with a family, joining in with their life, then the chances are that you will know some wonderful words like 'octopus' or 'telephone exchange', but you may never have the chance to pick up all the little everyday kitchen and garden words that are so necessary when you start expressing yourself. One way of helping learners with these sorts of words is by doing 'series vocabulary' warm-ups or fillers. The idea goes like this:

Procedure

Before class, choose a little area of life that involves a sequence of actions, e.g. making a phone call, making a cup of tea, going shopping, etc. Choose the level of vocabulary involved in the theme, for example, going for a walk in winter, at elementary level, *First you put on your coat, then you turn the lights off. Next you go out of the front door* . . . . But at advanced level, *First you get out an Ordnance Survey map and decide where to go. Next you get well wrapped up* . . . I think the best level to do this at is intermediate. Then some, but not all, of the words (nouns, prepositions and verbs) will be known already. Check with a native speaker if you are not too confident about the prepositions involved (e.g. *turn the lights off? out? down?*).

Then in class set the topic by bringing in some pictures, objects or sounds (e.g. if starting a car is your theme, bring in a tape of a car engine turning over).

1 Ask the learners to mime the sequence to each other so that it is well-established in their minds.
2 In a circle, ask one person to start the sequence with the words *First I* . . . and the next person to continue with *Then I* . . . or *Next I* . . . .
3 If you think all the words are likely to be new, then do one step each lesson, building up little by little, for example, wrapping a present: the first lesson might be, *First I choose something nice.* Then the second time you'd get someone to remember step one before going on to step two, *Next I get some wrapping paper.*

1.8

LEVEL
Intermediate +

EXTRAS
Realia (optional)

TIME
5 to 10 minutes

SKILLS FOCUS
Speaking and listening

Tessa Woodward

NOTE

The good thing about this idea is that learners can choose themes that are useful to them. (Don't forget, a sequence of actions is necessary). Preparation time is only about ten minutes before the start of a new sequence. All learners need this everyday language and it is hard to find in books. The idea can run forever and themes can be chosen to fit in with the topic of the work you are doing. Review time can involve learners writing out and drawing complete sequences and putting them on the wall or one person miming a sequence and everyone else shouting out the accompanying sentences. Another nice thing is that people tend to do things in different ways and this intrigues other people. If you have a class of good cooks, then 'making an omelette' will start off discussions of recipes. If you have a class of gardeners, then 'getting ready for spring in the garden' will involve them in idea swapping. Choosing something that you know little about will teach you something but you'll have to think fast to bring out the vocabulary the learners want.

1.9

LEVEL

Elementary + (better with intermediates and above)

EXTRAS

Paper or card and felt pens. A headline about a recent event in your life

TIME

5 to 10 minutes

SKILLS FOCUS

Mostly speaking and listening

Tessa Woodward

MAKING THE HEADLINES

For this idea you need some long pieces of thick paper or thin card and some thick felt tip pens. (One strip of paper/card and one pen for each learner).

Procedure

Before class, write out an example headline about yourself and your week or any event that's happened to you since you last saw your learners. My headline might be, 'TEACHER DIGS OLD CAR FROM BACK GARDEN', because my husband and I recently spent three days clearing old junk from the garden of our new house.

Then, in class, flash up your headline card to the class and invite them to ask you any questions they like, such as, *Was it a VW?* or *Was it in parts?* or *Is it true?*.

Then you give your learners time to think back over the past few days and to make a headline for themselves, too.

Two rules: each student's headline must be about them and it must relate to a real event although it can be an exaggeration of the facts, as mine was. When everyone has finished, the learners – in pairs, small groups, or all together – show each other their headlines. They can then ask each other any questions they like to get the whole of the story. Small groups (say fours) gives a nice balance between talking time and story variety.

RATIONALE

The good thing about this activity is that even elementary learners can usually manage short headlines like 'TERRIBLE WEEK' or 'GREAT SATURDAY IN ZURICH' and are usually glad to have a chance to leave out all the grammar for a change. More advanced learners can specialise in exaggerating the adjectives, selecting exciting verbs and showing off their knowledge of specialist vocabulary, for example, 'STUDENT DISCO SHOCK PROBE'. Just as importantly, everyone has a chance to express as little or as much as they want to about their recent past and to learn about their classmates' recent fortunes.

The activity can be used as an introductory warm-up to work on newspaper articles, or as a simple learning about each other exercise.

VARIATION

If you're brave, this activity could be adapted in order to gain feedback from learners on your lesson or course. You could bear 'FANTASTIC TEACHER THRILLS CLASS' but could you bear 'BORING, BORING, BORING!!'?

If you're not brave enough for this, keep the activity as a warm-up exercise. It's not often people get the chance to write their own headlines!

JUGGLING TENSES

1.10

Depending on the number and type of the flashcards the activity can take from five minutes (a little preview of coursework to follow) to twenty five minutes (everyone making example sentences and discussing them). Thus it can be a warm-up, a change, a pre-view, a review, or a substantial piece of work! This idea is useful for seeing what your learners are like at manipulating tenses.

LEVEL
Advanced

EXTRAS
Flashcards

TIME
5 to 25 minutes

Procedure

Before class, write some 'tense signposts' large and clear on pieces of white card. I mean lexis like *yesterday, just, after, tomorrow, at 4.30 pm on Monday, now, while.*

Then, in class:

1 Write a base sentence on the blackboard, such as, 'I went shopping at the new supermarket' or 'He finished his dinner'.

2 Explain to learners that as you flash up a card with a word on it they will have to alter the base sentence to fit that word in. Here's an example:

LANGUAGE FOCUS
Manipulation of verb forms

SKILLS FOCUS
Controlled speaking

Tessa Woodward

Base sentence: 'I went shopping at the new supermarket.' Teacher shows flashcard 'NEVER'. Learner says *I've never been shopping at that new supermarket.* Teacher shows flashcard 'OFTEN'. Learner says *I often go shopping at the new supermarket*, or *I often used to go there but I don't anymore.* (Both of these are fine).

3 Once learners have got the hang of the idea, just flash the cards up and see what they can produce.

RATIONALE

Even learners with a fair grasp of the tense system will find it a challenge to manipulate sentences at speed and the 'signpost' idea is a useful one. It's useful for non-native learners (and for would-be teachers!) to know that when certain words like *ever* come up, the range of options open to you in the sentence is immediately narrowed.

VARIATION

The scope of this activity can be widened out to include clauses. For example,

| 'but I changed my mind' | or | 'by the time I got home' | or | 'If I had done that . . .' |

I think I learnt this from Dilys Brown in the late 1970s.

1.11 GETTING INTO LINE

LEVEL
Elementary

EXTRAS
None

TIME
Less than 5 minutes

LANGUAGE FOCUS
Interaction language

SKILLS FOCUS
Speaking and listening

Tessa Woodward

You probably know some warm-up ideas involving learners lining up according to different rules and for different purposes. Perhaps there are one or two here that are new to you. Let's start with one that is good to do with a group who don't know each other well yet.

Procedure

1 Practise useful language, such as, *How do you spell your name?*, or *What's your name again?*, and, *L comes before N, so you go there.* Also, *R comes after P, so I'll stand here*, etc.

2 Mark a straight line or a horseshoe on the floor, with real or imaginary chalk. If you're using real chalk, draw an 'A' at one end and a 'Z' at the other – or use sheets of paper bearing an 'A' and a 'Z'.

3 Tell the class that each person should stand on the line where their first name goes in the alphabet. Check understanding by asking, for example, *Someone named Aaron would stand where? And Zoe . . . where? And Anna? Before or after Aaron? Why?*

4 Remind them of the language you had been practising earlier. Perhaps demonstrate how you can ask how someone spells their name and how you can tell them where they should stand in relation to you.

5 Say, *Go!*

RATIONALE

This line-up therefore practises useful social language as well as the memory of classmates' names and the alphabetising that is obviously necessary for dictionary use.

VARIATIONS

a Classes that know each other better can organise themselves by last names. Or you can ask each learner to think of someone special to them and then get into order according to the name of this person. When in line, people can chat for a bit about who they were thinking of and why they are special.

b Learners can order themselves according to the height of someone special to them. (There's not much language practice involved in getting into line according to their own height!)

c Learners can order themselves by birthday or by favourite season or time of day.

d Something different is to give each learner one of a group of words that makes one or more sentences. (You can whisper the word or give it on a slip of paper, but tell them not to show it!) Six words is generally the maximum.

  i Ask the learners to stand in a line – each person where their word belongs.

  ii When they're in order, ask them to get close to a neighbour if they're part of a contraction and stand well apart if they should be pronounced quite separately from their neighbours.

  iii Find out who has the most strongly stressed syllable in them.

  iv Be a 'choirmaster'. Have the learners say their words in the correct order and with as much natural contraction, linking, and stress as possible. The most stressed syllable can jump up in the air. This is good fun. In a larger class, you can give different groups different sets of words that can form related sentences.

e You can ask learners to suggest ways of ordering or let them prepare their own jigsaw sentences.

1.12

LEVEL
Elementary +

EXTRAS
Cards with matching pairs of pictures or words

TIME
10 minutes

LANGUAGE FOCUS
Vocabulary; interaction language

SKILLS FOCUS
Speaking and listening

Tessa Woodward

FINDING YOUR PARTNER

In one variation of this type of warm-up, you draw little houses on a set of strips of paper or pieces of card, such as in Fig. 3. Each picture needs one identical twin. They can differ from all the others by the position, number, colour of windows, chimneys, trees, flowers, etc. There should be, therefore, eight pairs of house cards in a room of sixteen students.

Fig. 3

Procedure

1 Show the class some sample pictures, some the same, some different. (Larger versions on A4 sheets can be shown or draw some on the board.)
2 Explain that in a couple of minutes each learner will have one picture and must stand up, walk around and find the other learner in the room who has a house and garden that looks exactly the same as hers or his.
3 Explain that they must talk in English. They must not look at any other person's card until they are sure that it's the same.
4 Practise the necessary language, for example:
   Has your house got a chimney?   *Yes, it has.*
   Has it got a door?   *No, it hasn't.*
   Where is it?   *It's in the sky/on the roof.*
   What colour is it?   *It's red/green ...*
   What shape is it?   *It's square/rectangular ...*
   It's the same (as mine)!
   It's different (from mine)!
5 Check understanding of the rules and start your class off.
6 Remember to tell them that the person who has the matching picture is their partner in what follows and so they should sit down together.

AIMS AND RATIONALE

The 'house picture' idea at elementary level practices basic house and colour vocabulary and prepositions plus *It's got.* Like any mingling activity it should involve practice of other useful interaction language like, *You first?, Sorry, I didn't get that, What do we do now?*, etc.

VARIATIONS

a The same cards (don't forget to take them back) can be used at higher levels with more sophisticated language, for example, *Would you like to describe your house to me?*, *OK, it's a rather charming little detached house standing in an acre of ground ...*

b As the basic idea behind this warm-up is simply finding a partner for some other activity, the cards need not have houses drawn on them. They can have language such as the two halves of a first conditional sentence, for example:

'If it rains...'   'I'll stay at home and watch telly.'

Fig. 4

Or words with matching stress patterns, for example:

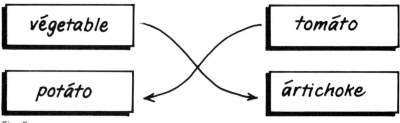

végetable   tomáto

potáto   ártichoke

Fig. 5

You can choose what to put on the cards according to what the following activity is that you want to pair learners up for.

NOTE

Whatever is on the cards, the learners have to search, verbally, for a partner. This means that the interaction language has to be elicited or taught and practised carefully each time.

For the vegetable cards above, the classroom language necessary would be, for example:

How do you say your word? I'll say my word. Is the stress the same? I'm not sure. Say it again.

The importance of dealing with the learners' need for this sort of language in activities like this cannot be stressed too much. Sometimes teachers fail to get the most out of communicative activities. We remember to practise the focus language (in other words, what's directly connected with what's on the cards), but forget to practise the interaction language (the language learners need to manage communicative encounters). As it happens, interactive language is very useful, often more useful than the focus language! Also, if you take it for granted that learners know it (but they don't), you may unwittingly be putting them in the position of having to use their mother tongue in order to accomplish the task you have set them. In other words, if they don't know how to say *Me first?* in English, they may say it in their own language. Or the activity may never get off the ground at all.

If interaction language is paid due attention, activities which involve finding a partner also practise the skill of approaching strangers or slight acquaintances and starting conversations. Most useful if you want to get served by a British barman.

1.13

LEVEL
Elementary +

EXTRAS
None

TIME
5 to 10 minutes

SKILLS FOCUS
Speaking and listening

Tessa Woodward

JUST ONE GOOD THING

Procedure

1 At the start of a class you ask learners to sit and think until they can find one positive thing that has happened to them so far in the day.
2 After a minute or so of thinking time has elapsed, start off by telling everyone about something good that has happened to you or something good that you noticed or heard about.
3 Invite learners to add their own anecdotes and tales. This can happen either one by one around the room (perhaps easier to start with) or with learners chipping in as they feel ready to.

This is a simple but beautiful warm-up idea I learned from a Spanish EFL teacher, Maria Luisa Martin Torres. When we tried it out in our group at the time, the contributions were mostly simple and everyday things, for example, a happy phone call, sunshine through a window, a cheerful greeting from a friend, tasty food, a glimpse of a cat .... The atmosphere at the end of the warm-up was very pleasant indeed. Looking around, people's faces were all light, enjoying, listening, smiling. A great way to start a learning period.

IN A PRISON CELL

Procedure

1 A group of four or five learners stand in a circle.
2 Explain that one person is in the middle trying to escape or get out of the circle. They can shout *Help!* or *Let me out!*. However, the people forming the circle must not let the captive out.
3 The first phase ends when a climax has been reached. The captive is released.
4 Four or five learners get cards with information on about name, crime, length of prison term, etc.,

1

| Name: Gilbert Jones |
| Crime: Murder |
| Sentence: Life imprisonment |

2

| Name: Thomas Fisher |
| Crime: Spy |
| Sentence: 20 years |

3

| Name: Kate Morgan |
| Crime: Selling Drugs |
| Sentence: 10 years |

4

| Name: Ellen Black |
| Crime: Squatting |
| Sentence: 1 year |

5 The rest of the learners get cards with their own names on them. These they pin to their clothes so that other learners can identify them.
6 The four criminals form a group and talk together about their lives but without saying what their crime is. They should mention the sentence as this is a vital hint.
7 The other learners – who are grouped around the criminals, eavesdropping – try to guess what crimes the criminals have committed.
8 After some minutes of conversation among the inmates, the rest of the learners may ask questions of the prisoners in order to guess their crimes. The prisoners can, again, talk about their crimes, but must not say specifically what their crimes are.
9 Once the activity is over, the teacher asks the learners to close their eyes and says:
Imagine you are in a forest, It's rather dark. You are walking towards a clearing. Now you see more light. The grass under your feet is soft. Now you have reached a beautiful meadow. You are walking across it. You feel like lying down on the grass. You stop and do it. Nothing worries you. A bird is singing. It's warm. You feel free and calm. You are free and happy.

1.14

LEVEL
Intermediate +

EXTRAS
Name cards and separate information cards

TIME
20 minutes

SKILLS FOCUS
Speaking and listening

Lucyna Adamus
Ida Baj-Sroda
Anna Fidzinsksa
Marek Konieczny
Hanna Wrzesien

1.15

LEVEL
Intermediate +

EXTRAS
None

TIME
5 to 10 minutes

Jim Wingate

GREETINGS

Procedure

1 Everyone circulates.
2 At a pre-arranged signal from you everyone stops and greets someone standing near to them.
3 They act and speak as if their partner is an old friend they haven't seen for ten years.
4 After a half a minute or so, you give another pre-arranged signal and everyone begins to mingle again.
5 Repeat this sequence two or three times.

VARIATIONS

a People greet each other as if they are old friends meeting, after a long time, at a ceremony where medals for bravery are being awarded.
b They are long-lost old friends greeting each other in a prison yard.
c Each time people stop circulating they act out a different situation.

1.16

LEVEL
Elementary to intermediate

EXTRAS
None

TIME
5 to 10 minutes

SKILLS FOCUS
Speaking, listening

Jim Wingate

CIRCLE STEP

Procedure

1 Everyone forms a circle with enough room between people for everyone to take one step forward.
2 One person enters the circle and says something relating to a chosen topic, such as a poem or story that was recently done in class.
3 Everyone in the circle takes one step forward, repeats what has just been said, and then steps back again.
4 A new person replaces the previous person in the circle and says something else on the topic, and so forth.

VARIATIONS

a After repeating what someone has said, the people in the circle applaud noisily.
b Successive people in the circle alternate between saying what girls say to boys and boys to girls, what learners say to teachers and teachers to learners, what parents say to children and children to parents . . . .

THE ROOM AS A MAP

1.17

Exactly how this works, depends on where in the world you are and where in the world your learners come from. Let's suppose they come from Europe and the Mediterranean coast of Africa.

LEVEL
Elementary +

EXTRAS
None

Procedure

TIME
5 minutes

1 Say that your room is going to be Europe and Northern Africa.
2 Point to the floor on the northernmost side of your room. Ask where that is. *Spitzbergen* is a good answer, but settle for *Norway* or *Sweden.* Establish the other three points of the compass in a similar way.

SKILLS FOCUS
Speaking and listening

3 Ask everyone to think of a place that they can go to in any of the countries now in the room ... a place they have really been to in their lives, a place that is special to them for some reason. It cannot be where they live now. It should not be where they were born, unless it is special to them for some other reason too.

Seth Lindstromberg

4 Say that in a minute they should walk to this place, stop, and stand ... and that everyone should then ask one or two people standing near them where they are and why that place is special to them.
5 People will have to do a fair amount of talking before a consensus is reached on what is where in the middle of the floor, but this usually happens spontaneously.

VARIATIONS

a The room can be a map of anywhere and people can stand in places for all kinds of reasons.
b The perimeter of the room can be the rim of a clock.
  i People go to the hour of the day they like best.
  ii When they get there, they ask someone near them whether they are at X o'clock AM or PM and find out why they like that time and what they do then.
c The perimeter of the room can be the cycle of the seasons of the year.
d The perimeter of the room is the last 5,000 years.

ACKNOWLEDGEMENT

I learned this activity from Judith Baker in 1985.

1.18

LEVELS
Elementary to
lower-intermediate

EXTRAS
None

TIME
5 minutes

**LANGUAGE
FOCUS**
Asking questions

SKILLS FOCUS
Speaking and
listening

*Lindsay
Brown Dixey*

THE ANSWER IS 'YES', THE ANSWER IS 'NO'

I'll describe this activity as it can be used to practise the simple past form of questions.

Procedure

1 Tell your learners to shout out questions using the simple past, to which you can honestly reply *Yes*. For example:

LEARNER 1: Did you watch TV last night?
TEACHER: Yes.
LEARNER 2: Did you brush your teeth last night?
TEACHER: Yes.

2 If a learner asks you a question to which you would honestly give *No* as a reply, the learner is either eliminated from the session, given a forfeit at the end of the class, or made to ask another question.

3 If a learner asks a question which is grammatically incorrect, again the learner can either be eliminated, or made to ask another question or the teacher can show a flashcard 'HELP!' to the rest of the class so that the learner can correct their question.

VARIATIONS

a After a couple of minutes, repeat the same procedure with questions to which you can answer, *No.*

b i The learners ask questions involving particular sounds or new vocabulary. For |i| questions could be *Did you sleep well?* or *Did you have meat for supper?*

   ii After answering the question, ask the other learners to repeat the word with |i| in it.

c Other cards you can flash to indicate errors could be:

 Which means *time* or *tense* and tells a learner that they need to correct the tense in what they have just said.

 Which means *intonation* or *melody* and tells a learner to repeat what they have just said but not in a monotone.

 Which means that they have not formed a question properly, that is, they have omitted a necessary *do* or have neglected to swap the subject and the first auxiliary.

You can also have the flashcards stuck on the wall and point to them.

d A learner can take the place of the teacher and answer the questions.

e The learners can prepare their questions at home.

CORNER CARDS

Procedure

1.19

LEVEL
Lower
intermediate +

EXTRAS
Filing cards

TIME
20 to 30 minutes the
first time, then 5 to 10
minutes each time

SKILLS FOCUS
Speaking and
listening

***Seth
Lindstromberg***

1 Explain the difference between the title and the sub-title of a book, for example, 'Car Racing: the least comprehensible sport' or '1815: the year of Waterloo'.

2 Then, write something like this on the board:

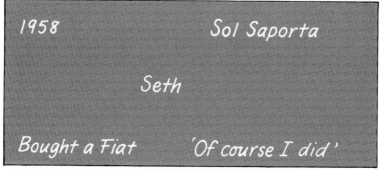

Fig. 6

3 Say that each of the things you've written at the corners is the title of a book you could write, but haven't yet.

4 Invite your learners to ask you questions to discover the 'sub-title' of each of these four 'book titles'. The questions should not be yes/no questions only. Any question is allowed except, *What's the sub-title?* You may want to give them your first sub-title as an example – mine is '1958: A year in which there was a big change in my life'
And ask your class what questions would get this answer from you. For example, *Was that when you were born?* doesn't work because you only answer *Yes. Was that a special year for you?* is a bit better but a question that does gets you to divulge the sub-title and more, is *Why was 1958 special for you?* Even, *Why have you written 1958?* Interestingly, your learners may have played so many games in which only *yes/no* questions were allowed that they may be wary of being so natural and direct. And this is part of what everyone's going to practise.

(My other sub-titles are: Sol Saporta — Someone who influenced me in a very positive way. Bought a cheap second hand Fiat — Something I shouldn't have done. *Of course I did* — Something I said that got me into trouble).

5 Once the students have guessed the sub-titles of your books, invite them to ask you a stipulated number of questions, say five, to find more out about what each book would have in it. Again, *Wh-* questions are allowed too. Also, learners can pursue any topic that comes up with a separate line of questioning leading far away from the original focus. Surprisingly, it may take your students a while to realise how much freedom they have in this regard. In any case, you may all be amazed at how much they can find out about you in a short time.

6 Give each learner a filing card and ask them to write four book titles in each corner and their first name or a nickname they'd like to be known by in the centre. The sub-titles must be the same and in the same corners, but the book titles must be different.

7 Point out a couple of conditions: In the top left corner they can't put the year they were born or the year they got married. In the top right corner they cannot put any member of their immediate family. In the bottom left corner they can only put *Come here* if they dare!

8 When everyone has finished their cards (this should take from three to five minutes), put them into pairs and ask them to swap cards.

9 Ask them to ask each other a minimum of ten questions about the top left item ONLY. First one learner does the interviewing and then the other. Tell them that each learner must make a little tick on their partner's card, in the appropriate corner, for every question they ask. Keeping score seems to encourage the least motivated learners to get into the activity. Don't make a big deal of this if talk is flowing well anyway.

10 When most learners have asked their ten questions to their partner (you can tell by counting the ticks), break off the activity, and collect the cards.

11 You can use the cards more than once by doing only one corner per time and/or by pairing people differently.

VARIATIONS

a Sub-titles can be varied, for example, 'something I'd like to be able to do but which I can't', 'the nicest place I've ever lived or stayed' ... (Typical EFL topics like 'my favourite hobby' are too tedious and don't work well).

You can find titles/sub-titles which encourage use of particular verb forms though the simple past is easiest to practise in a sustained way.

In a Business English class, topics can be chosen that include practice of more specialised language, such as, 'my most time-consuming responsibility', 'what I would like to have further training in', etc.

b I have used this activity on a few occasions as a complete first, 'getting acquainted' lesson by asking learners to go through all four corners. On a Royal Society of Arts Certificate in TEFL course I paired trainees with their volunteer learners to get them relating to each other more informally. When it was time to finish 90 minutes later, everyone was still talking avidly.

NOTE

You will find that very few learners can refer correctly to the various corners and will produce terms like *right up corner*. A bit of drilling on this point is rarely amiss.

I learned this activity from Tessa Woodward who learned it from Clive Jacques at The International Language Centre, Kanda, Tokyo.

WALLS

Procedure

1 Lead learners through a visualisation phase as follows:

Imagine you are a wall ... Where are you?
Inside (what room?) or outside?
What material are you made of?
What colour are you? – painted or wallpapered or natural? – plain or patterned?
What would you like on you? – pictures? (which?) – posters? – flying ducks?
What would you like against you / and/or near you?
There are certain marks upon you – stains, scratches, the scars of life ... Where are they? How did you get them?

2 In pairs, learners discuss the walls they visualised.
3 As a whole class, discuss walls in your life (real, physical, abstract, mental). Try to find similarities/ differences between those walls.
4 Suggested material for further work: the poem, 'Mending Wall' by Robert Frost; the songs 'Close to it All' by Melanie or 'Another Brick in the Wall' by Pink Floyd.

A version of this activity is to be found in *Visual Impact*, David A. Hill's book in this series on using pictures.

Mending Wall [1914]

Something there is that doesn't love a wall,
That sends the frozen-ground-swell under it,
And spills the upper boulders in the sun;
And makes gaps even two can pass abreast.
The work of hunters is another thing:
I have come after them and made repair
Where they have left not one stone on a stone,
But they would have the rabbit out of hiding,
To please the yelping dogs. The gaps I mean,
No one has seen them made or heard them made,
But at spring mending-time we find them there.
I let my neighbor know beyond the hill;
And on a day we meet to walk the line
And set the wall between us once again.
We keep the wall between us as we go.
To each the boulders that have fallen to each.
And some are loaves and some so nearly balls
We have to use a spell to make them balance:
'Stay where you are until our backs are turned!'
We wear our fingers rough with handling them.

1.20

LEVEL
Intermediate

EXTRAS
Optional, the poem 'Mending Wall', by Robert Frost

TIME
10 to 15 minutes

SKILLS FOCUS
Listening; speaking; optional reading or listening

Sheelagh Deller
David A Hill

Oh, just another kind of outdoor game,
One on a side. It comes to little more:
There where it is we do not need the wall:
He is all pine and I am apple orchard.
My apple trees will never get across
And eat the cones under his pines, I tell him.
He only says, 'Good fences make good neighbors.'
Spring is the mischief in me, and I wonder
If I could put a notion in his head:
'*Why* do they make good neighbors? Isn't it
Where there are cows? But here there are no cows.
Before I built a wall I'd ask to know

What I was walling in or walling out,
And to whom I was like to give offense.
Something there is that doesn't love a wall,
That wants it down.' I could say 'Elves' to him,
But it's not elves exactly, and I'd rather
He said it for himself. I see him there
Bringing a stone grasped firmly by the top
In each hand, like an old-stone savage armed.
He moves in darkness as it seems to me,
Not of woods only and the shade of trees.
He will not go behind his father's saying,
And he likes having thought of it so well
He says again, 'Good fences make good neighbors.'

Robert Frost

CHAPTER 2

Accuracy: getting it right

This chapter contains activities which focus on getting language exactly right in one or more of its aspects. There are activities here for helping your learners to get the grammar right, the spelling, the punctuation, and the pronunciation. There are a number of activities to help them hear more detail. Connections between forms of language and their meanings are not neglected either!

UNPACKING A SENTENCE

Short newspaper articles are ideal for this activity, for example, 'News in Brief' items. Short stories in magazines like *Reader's Digest* often start with a suitable sentence containing a lot of information. Here are two examples:

CIA Chief Critical

Mr William Casey, the former CIA head, was in a critical condition yesterday at the Glen Cove Community Hospital in a suburb of New York, a hospital spokesman said.
The Times, 27th April, 1987

A

Cat's feat – A 16-week-old kitten named Mor jumped 200 feet from a balcony of her 22nd-floor apartment in British Columbia to the street and walked away without a scratch.
The Guardian, 9th June, 1987

B

2.1

LEVEL
Elementary +

EXTRAS
A few long sentences that you have 'unpacked' before

TIME
15 to 45 minutes

SKILLS FOCUS
Reading and writing or speaking

Jane and Dave Willis

Procedure

1 Ask your learners to read one sentence and think about what information it gives them.
2 Then ask them to write as many true sentences as they can (or you may set a certain number of sentences). These sentences must be based on the information given in the sentence they have read.

Learners might write the following sentences based on example sentence A:

Mr William Casey used to be head of the CIA. He was seriously ill. He was in a critical condition. He was in hospital. The name of the hospital was Glen Cove Community Hospital. It's in a suburb of New York. The news was reported by a hospital spokesman.

Shorter sentences drawn from the ideas in sentence B might be:
The kitten's name was Mor. There was once a kitten whose name was Mor. It was 16-weeks-old. It was a female kitten. She lived in an apartment. The apartment was in British Columbia. The apartment was 22 floors up. It had a balcony. The kitten jumped off the balcony. She landed in the street. She walked away. She was not hurt at all.

3 Let learners, in pairs or fours, read each others' sentences, compare, and comment. This is the stage at which you might want to help them correct any mistakes. Encourage learners to improve or correct each others' sentences.
4 Ask students in turn to read out a sentence to the rest of the class. They can see how many others wrote the same sentences and who got the most different ones.

RATIONALE

This is a good exercise because the actual writing is simple, but it requires detailed and accurate comprehension of the text. It makes learners aware of the structure of complex sentences, and the relationships between groups of words. It's great fun to do in class, too, especially with learners working in pairs.

This activity works very well with adult remedial beginners, but you need to choose simpler sentences.

VARIATIONS

a Ask learners to bring in a new items themselves, then you or the class can choose ones which have long and/or complex sentences.
b Get a more advanced class to select some suitable news stories for an intermediate class and produce a list of sentences as a key for the intermediates to check against.
c Pair learners off. Set a time limit and see which pair can write the most sentences. (Try the time limit out with another teacher first, then adjust it a bit, but not too much to remove the challenge.)
d Give the long sentence as a dictation.
e Before you give the sentence, write three or four key words on the board and get learners to guess what the sentence is about.
f Instead of simple sentences, ask learners to write as many questions as they can – questions that can be answered from the long sentence.
g Learners do the unpacking orally.

The inspiration for this 'unpacking' exercise was a lecture given by Professor Michael Halliday in Singapore.

REPACKING A SENTENCE
Procedure

2.2

LEVEL
Elementary +

EXTRAS
Short sentences for
'repacking'

TIME
15 to 45 minutes

SKILLS FOCUS
Reading and,
especially, writing

*Jane and Dave
Willis*

Either – Take a complex sentence from a news item, like the ones in the previous activity, *Unpacking a Sentence*, and break it down into a series of short simple sentences. Write these sentences on the board or dictate them. The sentence you choose for breaking down should be from a text that the learners have read before, otherwise the task to come could be frustratingly difficult.

Or – Ask learners to do some unpacking (see the previous activity), writing their sentences neatly on a piece of paper, which they exchange with another learner.

1 Without looking back at the original text, ask learners to put all the information that is in their lists of short sentences back into one long sentence. Allow learners to work in pairs and help each other.

There will usually be several different ways of combining the bits of information. For the sentences given below:

There is a train service connecting Euston with Holyhead. It is an express train service. It travels at 60mph. A man was arrested last night. It is thought he had been walking on the roof of the train, *one possible way might be:* A man who had supposedly been walking on the roof of the 60mph express train that runs between Euston and Holyhead was arrested last night., *rather than the original:* A man was arrested last night after allegedly walking on the roof of the Holyhead-Euston 60mph express train.' [*The Daily Telegraph* 21 January, 1987]

2 Help the learners to express themselves and get their version accurate.
3 Learners write their final sentences on an OHP transparency, or on the blackboard. Alternatively, learners read out their sentences and compare with each other's. Are there any differences in meaning or emphasis?
4 Learners compare their versions with the original. (Their versions may even be better!)

VARIATION

Revision lesson – unpacking and repacking.
Choose some complex sentences from texts you want learners to read again for revision purposes. Try to collect enough sentences for the whole class. Write these out on separate bits of paper.
1 Give one sentence to each learner or pair of learners.
2 Learners each unpack their own sentence, writing their list of short sentences on a separate piece of paper. They add a headline or title.
3 Check this work as they write to make sure it is accurate.
4 Take in the original complex sentences and keep them.
5 Learners pass their unpacked sentences round the class, for each learner or pair to repack in turn. If you have a big class, specify the number of sentences learners should aim to repack.

6 Display everyone's repacked sentences around the walls for learners to compare.

7 Tell the class which texts the original sentences came from. Then ask your learners to find these sentences in the texts (for useful skimming practice) and compare their version with the original. They could do this for homework.

Once you have chosen your sentences, this makes a very simple but satisfying lesson, in which your learners are working much harder than you! All you have to do is help them to express themselves clearly and accurately. Don't forget to keep your copies of the original sentences for another class.

For more examples and more detailed exploitation of the actual grammar involved in unpacking and repacking, see the *Collins Cobuild English Course*, (Jane and Dave Willis 1989, Level 3, Sections 50, 142, 150, 155, 165, and 189).

2.3

LEVEL
Lower
intermediate +

EXTRAS
None

TIME
10 to 30 minutes

SKILLS FOCUS
All four

*Jean-Paul
Creton*

DOWN TO ONE WORD

Procedure

1 Present one or two long sentences or series of shorter ones on the board, for example:

'No one at Lydd-on-Sea was staring out the window at the hideous nuclear power station and whispering, 'God help us', but rather the general activity had to do with tidying. I thought about this as I walked along, and it seemed hugely appropriate that people were ironing antimacassars in a spot where a nuclear meltdown could be occurring. This was England, after all.'

Paul Theroux *The Kingdom by the Sea* Penguin 1984 p. 52

2 Pair your learners up. Tell them that in a couple of minutes they are going to try to reduce this sentence to one word before their partner does.

3 Tell them they will take it in turns.

4 Explain that they may take out one word, two words, or three words when it is their turn. Stress that two or three words can be taken out only if they are consecutive.

5 Demonstrate how this works by reducing a shorter trial sentence on the board. Elicit suggestions from the class. Don't forget to insist all necessary changes in punctuation are specified, as when shorter sentences are created from a longer one.

6 Explain that each time it is their turn and they make a reduction, they

must read their new, shorter passage to their partner to show that they have left a correct and a complete sentence. Only then is it their partner's turn.

7 If someone's partner does not accept the reduction, they must call you since you are the referee!

8 Again, after each learner has read their new reduced passage, it is partner's turn. Remember, whoever reduces the passage to a single word that makes sense by itself wins.

EDITOR'S NOTE

I have tried dozens of different sentences and texts with different classes and it has always been possible to reach a one word sentence through a series of perfectly grammatical reductions. It does help, from time to time, to ask people to paraphrase a reduction that has a meaning that not everyone can see or to ask for a context in which someone might say what results from a suggested reduction.

AUTHOR'S NOTE

This is, of course, a version of John Morgan and Mario Rinvolucri's *Silent Sentence* (*Once Upon A Time* 1983 pp 98–101). But note how wonderfully well I've turned it into a competition for pairs and made it noisy!

AS IF ENGLISH

2.4

The procedure described here can work between any two languages. English and French are used as examples.

Procedure

1 Teach the following pronunciation 'code' in which, for example, the letters *ay* should always be pronounced as in the word *day*, etc.

ay = day	ee = see
igh = high	oa = boat
ar = car	air = chair
a = apple	or = for
ir = bird	ull = gull
oo = too	ort = port
y = you	sh = shut
er = never	k = kiss
e = bed	j = John
ng = sing (with silent 'g')	o = not

Most of the combinations of letters always have the pronunciation indicated, the others often do. So what learners are working on here is valuable in itself.

LEVEL
Beginner +

EXTRAS
Handouts of the 'code' and the two texts

TIME
10 to 20 minutes each time

LANGUAGE FOCUS
Pronunciation

SKILLS FOCUS
All four

REQUIREMENT
A monolingual class

Jenny Vanderplank

Canadians, Irish, most Scots and American teachers will need to adapt this system to account for the fact they pronounce /r/ after vowels.

2 Encourage your learners to speak in a very English way. In other words, encourage them to over-act and try to sound as ridiculously English as possible. (To straighten a steel rod you may have to bend it twice as far the other way as you want it to end up. Pronunciation exercises can work the same way.)

3 Ask learners, in pairs, to read aloud the text you have encoded. The example text here, 'La Cigale et La Fourmi' ('The Cicada and the Ant' – a West African adaptation of a well-known fable by La Fountaine), is for French speakers. Below is the encoded text for use with your class.

Lar *See*gull Ay Lar *For*mee

Lar *see*gull ar *sharn*tay too *lay*tay, may lar *for*mee ellar tra*vigh*ay doo. Kang *Pee*ver ay venoo, lar *see*gull navay *ploo ree*nar *marn*jay. Ellay*tall*ay *vwar* lar *for*mee ay el *looee* ar de *marn*day delar *nooree too*. Lar *for*mee ar dee *noa*! La *see*gull ay *mort. Sar*nay fai*ree*yan, la *for*mee ay *mort*oasee! Lar mor*arl* de set*eest*war *ay*: 'See too *manj* oo *see* too ne *marn*j *par*, too *krev* kom*aym*!

Here is the real French version (not for use with your class).

La cigale a chantée tout l'ete, mais la fourmi, elle a travaillé dur. Quand l'hiver est venu, la cigale n'avait plus rien à manger. Elle est allée voir la fourmi et elle lui a demandé de la nourriture. La fourmi a dit 'non'! La cigale est morte. Cela ne fait rien. La fourmi est morte aussi.

La morale de cette histoire est 'Si tu manges ou si tu ne manges pas, tu crèves quand même'.

When reading the encoded text, your learners will not at first grasp the sense of what they are reading. (Remember, in this case, they are native speakers of French). As the hidden story slowly emerges, there are always shrieks of laughter.

4 The learners continue to practise reading the French as if it were English, using the code as a guide. (Again, they are also learning the real English sound values of the various letters of the alphabet and their various combinations). This practice can be led by you for the whole group at once, done in pairs, or done individually. If it is done individually, ask your learners to whisper 'dramatically'.

5 Learners read, with the same exaggeration, an encoded English text. (That is, er text writtern lighk this). For many, the 'exaggeration' will be the best English you've ever heard them speak!

6 Learners transcribe the encoded English text into real English.

You can use this technique with any sort of text. Of course, for some other language, you may have to extend the code given in step 1. This exercise could give you useful insights into problems faced by your learners in reading English.

VARIATIONS

a Ask your learners to encode mother tongue texts of their own choice such as jokes or news items. This can be done as homework. Then, learners read their texts out to the whole group. Ham acting is essential!

b **i** Ask learners which of them feel more like ants and which feel more like cicadas.

ii In pairs they prepare, then act out a sketch of the cicadas' visit to the ant. They can act it out as they like. The results are usually hilarious and often surprising. Some ants are very kind and some cicadas are really awful.

iii All the ants meet and tell each other about their experiences with the cicadas who came knocking on their doors. The cicadas also exchange news.

WEAK FORMS DICTATION
Procedure

1 Dictate disconnected sentences or a short passage. (As ever, try to use interesting material).
2 Ask the learners to write only the auxiliary verbs they hear – each one on a different line.
3 Then ask learners to ask questions using the auxiliaries they have noted down. They should use as many different question words as possible.
4 To deal with meaning, try to answer or get other learners to answer every question no matter how bizarre or unusual it might be.
5 Use the learners' questions in a burst of intensive drilling. The aim is to get learners saying the questions with the auxiliaries naturally weakened and liaised, e.g. *Whatəryou DOing?*

EDITOR'S NOTE

Sheelagh has written another book in this series, *Lessons From the Learner*, which presents activities that involve learners creating their own practice material.

2.5

LEVEL
Lower elementary to intermediate

EXTRAS
None

TIME
5 to 15 minutes

LANGUAGE FOCUS
Unstressed auxiliaries

SKILLS FOCUS
Intensive listening, controlled speaking ... some writing

Sheelagh Deller

2.6

LEVEL

Beginner +

EXTRAS

A text for dictation

TIME

Depends on the length of the text dictation

SKILLS FOCUS

Intensive reading, speaking

Tessa Woodward

THE RUNITALLTOGETHER DICTATION

Procedure

1 Hand out a run-together text.
2 The learners put slashes (/) between words. They do this individually or in consultation with neighbours.
3 The learners read the text back to the teacher who writes it up on the OHP or blackboard.
4 You do several things:
   a Ask questions, e.g. How do you spell *their*?
   b Act like a computer saying, e.g. *Bleep! Will not accept!*
   c Write down exactly what learners say and how they say it including all mistakes. The learners orally correct your transcription. You must insist that they be specific. Remember, computers do only what they are told to do. The aim here is to encourage your learners to form familiar suggestions and practise such text correction terminology as *Change the a to an e*. Your learners won't be forced to come to grips with this language if you anticipate their wishes. So act really stupid.
   d Put in the slashes where learners say and let the group vote on whether the locations are correct.

I learnt this from Elio my German teacher in Switzerland. A similar idea is described in an article by Jan van den Bos in *Practical English Teaching* (March 1983).

ALTERATION DICTATIONS
Procedure

1 Dictate a single sentence.
2 Each learner has to write the sentence changing the wording as much as possible while changing the meaning as little as possible, e.g.:

TEACHER   Diamonds are the hardest substance known to man.
LEARNER A   Diamonds are the hardest material known to men and women.
LEARNER B   A diamond is harder than anything else known to humanity.

3 Stress that learners should not at any time write the sentence you have read out but should only write their altered one. Some will try to take down your sentences and change them later. It seems to me that this makes it possible for learners to do the exercise without mentally processing what they hear deeply enough for learning to be fostered as well as it might be.
4 Ask learners to read out their adaptations after each of the first two sentences in order to make sure everyone understands the rules.
5 Read out the rest of your sentences, or the rest of your text. Then pool the different versions of each of your sentences, discussing, in particular, the degree to which each varies in meaning from the original.

VARIATIONS

a Give most kudos for a change of one word only.
b Maximum change in meaning about the same theme without use of *not*, *no*, or *none*.

These ideas came to me after a workshop on creative dictations given by Mario Rinvolucri in 1985.

2.7

LEVEL
Elementary +

EXTRAS
Suitable texts or lists of sentences

TIME
10 to 15 minutes

LANGUAGE FOCUS
Expressing identical or similar concepts in various ways

SKILLS FOCUS
Intensive listening, writing, speaking

Seth Lindstromberg

2.8

LEVEL
Intermediate

EXTRAS
A list of restrictive or non-restrictive relative clauses; all on one theme

TIME
30 to 45 minutes

LANGUAGE FOCUS
Aural discrimination of restrictive and non-restrictive clauses

SKILLS FOCUS
Intensive listening, writing, controlled speaking

Seth Lindstromberg

THE EARTH AND WHIZBANGO

This activity is a challenging follow-on to work on restrictive vs non-restrictive relative clauses.

Procedure

1 Discuss the earth, sun, moon and planets, as well as poles, climactic zones and so forth. Alternatively, assign a suitable reading, perhaps from a children's encyclopedia like *Collier's* or *The World Book Encyclopedia*. Or do both. However you manage this phase, establish the basic facts concerning the earth's place in the solar system and its global geography.

2 Describe the planet Whizbango. It has several moons and two suns. Amazingly, it has two quite different atmospheres, one for each hemisphere and they hardly mix at all. Not only that, but there are two magnetic axes, one running north-south (along the principal axis of rotation) like the Earth's, the other running in a different direction. Also, because there are two suns, there are two different equators; but because the suns are of different intensity and not equally close, only one equatorial belt is tropical. In other respects, though, the two planets (and their solar systems) are virtually identical.

3 Ask your learners to sketch pictures of Whizbango and its suns and moons. Let them compare their drawings.

4 Read out the following statements (or others you can think of). Learners write them either on the top or bottom halves of their sheets of paper, depending on whether these statements are true of the Earth (top) or Whizbango (bottom). Mention that the statements have been selected from a respected galactic tourist guidebook and each is true of either our planet or Whizbango, but no statement is true of both planets, even though important facts may be the same.

The sun which rises in the east is generally a bright, pale yellow.
The atmosphere, which has a certin amount of oxygen in it, is clear when conditions are ideal.
The moon, which appears to have different shapes at different times, is devoid of life.
The equatorial zone which is quite hot at sea level includes both deserts, jungle and oceans.
The magnetic poles which are near the polar ice caps are strong enough to aid in navigation
The morning star, which is also the evening star, is not really a star at all. It's another planet.
The evening star which is brighter than any real star can also be clearly seen at dawn.
The sun, which can be painfully bright, is, on average, about 93 million miles distant.
The moon which you can sometimes see in the daytime seems to have a face on it when it's full.

The sun, which bombards the planet with all sorts of radiation, is an average sort of star, though a bit on the small side.

5 Ask your learners to compare their answers then go through the sentences with the whole class. Constantly link the difference in how the sentences are read to the difference in meaning.
6 Drill learners on saying some of the sentences.
7 Put the learners in groups. Ask each one to read some of their sentences to the rest of their group who try to guess from the way it is said whether the reader was trying to say a sentence belonging on the top half of their sheet or one for the bottom half. In this way, each learner gets some immediate feedback on whether they can say what they really mean or whether they're saying something they don't mean!

NOTE

The original dictation seems best done as a 'learner power' dictation. This is a dictation in which learners are encouraged to use language like *Wait, What was that again?* and so forth. This is because you should be speaking at normal conversational speed, which, though it is necessary for authenticity, is likely to be difficult for some learners to cope with. See *Models and Metaphors in Language Teacher Training* (*Woodward* 1990)

VARIATION

Obviously if you think your class may not be interested in planets and so forth, you can develop a different pair of related topics.

SOUND POEMS

2.9

PREPARATION

Choose a short poem and lead the learners in practise of how to read it in different ways, using different techniques, for example pausing for effect; stressing certain words heavily (i.e. prolonging the stressed syllable varying loudness and softness by whispering and shouting different parts of the poem; experimenting with speed — starting slo-o-o-o-wly). The poem can be read over and over, each time faster and faster.

Practice in the skill of reading a poem out loud is vital in stages 3 and 4. Reading a short poem, as above, will prepare the group for this experience.

LEVEL
Intermediate +

EXTRAS
The list of questions and a short poem

TIME
30 to 60 minutes

SKILLS FOCUS
All four

Bonnie Tsai

Procedure

1 Present the questions on the facing page. To do this, supply handouts, use on OHP, record the questions to listen to in a language lab, etc.

2 Learners write down the answers one after the other from top to bottom along the left hand side of a piece of paper. They answer using phrases of three to five words or in three to five key words that do not make phrases. Full sentences are not allowed, but if a question stymies a learner, they can skip it.

3 Tell the learners that they have all written poems. And explain that they are now going to read their poems out loud to the class.

4 Give them some time to prepare, perhaps by going off to various corners of the room or into the corridor to 'whisper-rehearse' their poem after marking the words they want to stress. They may want to practise reading it in different ways, as in the preparation phase.

VARIATION

If they are in the language lab, learners can practise the poem by recording themselves on cassette. They can re-record themselves until they are satisfied with their rendition. Later, they play their favourite versions to the whole class. Here's one example of an answer poem:

Poem Of The Answers

Soft rhythms on tin
Torrents of mini wetness
Odour spray
Spreading; pushing, never toe touching ground
Twisting strands – sometimes silky flowing, oil
Smooth body surface
Filled with dread anticipation
Moist flower fragrance
A burning cold

Wet heat, when first to breathe is dying
In fresh clearance objects sparkle and air is pure
A finely never broken woven texture
Sharp, bumpy pains against the pad of feet
Dry dampness underneath
Bare top dry
Blue crystals on tongue
All perfection, soaring through air with wings
Outstretched, silhouetted against the cloud

ACKNOWLEDGEMENT

The Art of Subversive Teaching: Teaching as a Subversive Activity (Postman and Weingartner 1977).

1 What do you hear if you are in a car and it is raining outside?

2 What do you feel if you are standing outside in the rain?

3 How does gasoline (petrol) smell to you?

4 What sounds do you hear if you are walking in heavy boots in deep snow?

5 Think of someone you know. Think of their hair. What does it feel like?

6 How would you describe the texture of skin?

7 Have you ever felt afraid? How does it feel?

8 How would you describe the odour of freshly cut grass?

9 Is there a particular odour in the air before rainfall? Describe it.

10 Is there a particular odour in the air after rainfall? Describe it.

11 If your hand slides across a piece of silk, what sensation do you feel?

12 If you were to walk barefoot along a beach of pebbles, what sensation would you feel?

13 What does the palm of your hand feel like?

14 What does someone else's palm feel like?

15 Can you describe the taste of the sea?

16 How would you describe the flight of a seagull?

CHAPTER 3

Role plays

A teacher is asked, *Do you use role plays in class?*, and replies, *Of course I do. They're part of the landscape, like books and chalk. Jacques is the policeman and Yvette the lady tourist trying to find the railway station. I spent three hours last night making role cards for them. Jacques was very good – he used lots of conditionals and got most of them right.*

No, I'm not knocking traditional classroom role plays; most learners like them (for a while at least) and they give a needed opportunity for practising particular functions and structures. What they lack, though, is content: the sort of content that engages the full attention of those involved. The following activities, which owe much to psychodrama, attempt to remedy this lack. They are all, in their way, role plays.

All may be done in large or small groups.

John Morgan

3.1

LEVEL
Beginner +

EXTRAS
One dialogue with one word exchanges

TIME
Phase One, 5 minutes for each variation
Phase Two, 20 to 30 minutes

LANGUAGE FOCUS
Intonation from word to sentence level

SKILLS FOCUS
Speaking and listening

Sheelagh Deller

INTONATION DIALOGUES

Intonation seems to be an area which frightens teachers and is undervalued by language learners. Yet it is an aspect of language which can generate interesting, valuable, and realistic interaction. Perhaps one reason why we shy away from intonation work is its complexity. Where do we start? One answer is to start at word level.

Procedure

PHASE ONE:

1 Pair off the learners.
2 Tell them they are going to have a conversation in which they:
   a greet each other as long lost friends
   b have an argument
   c make friends again
3 Tell them that the only words they can use for this are the numbers one to fifty, e.g.,

   LEARNER A (enthusiastically) 1, 2, 3, 4, 5!
   LEARNER B (surprised) 6, 7, 8!

4 Explain that each learner carries on 'counting' where their partner stopped.

RATIONALE

This activity allows learners to focus only on intonation and, because of its simplicity, can be done at all levels. Learners are amused and encouraged to realise that they can transmit so much information by intonation alone.

VARIATIONS

a Use only one word, e.g. *Susan.*
b One learner uses *yes* and the other *no.*
c Use words of a well known rhyme, e.g., 'Sing a song of sixpence'.

PHASE TWO:

From word level it is then easier to move into sentence level, and for this, ambiguous dialogues are an excellent source of material and quite easy to create.

Here is an example dialogue for all learners to use:

LEARNER A	What shall we do?
LEARNER B	Sorry
LEARNER A	What shall we do?
LEARNER B	I don't know
LEARNER A	Do you mind?
LEARNER B	I don't know what to say.
LEARNER A	Why?
LEARNER B	It's so difficult
LEARNER A	I know

1 Ask learners to read the dialogue silently.
2 Ask global questions, e.g., *Is it day or night?, What sex are the speakers?, How do they feel about each other?, What's their problem?.*
3 Ask different learners to read line 1. Ask other learners to react to HOW it was said. To do this you ask such questions as, *Is he/she sincere?, Why did he/she say that?, or What mood is he/she in?.*
4 Put the learners in pairs.
5 Give them time to decide who they are, where they are, and what they are talking about. Ask them to learn the dialogue by heart and prepare to act it out to other pairs who must guess the situation.

I got the idea for Phase One from Cynthia Beresford. There is a similar activity on p. 113 of *Drama Techniques in Language Learning (Maley and Duff, 1982).*

3.2

LEVEL
Beginner +

EXTRAS
None

TIME
45 to 60 minutes
without the
extension

**LANGUAGE
FOCUS**
Numbers,
vocabulary,
intonation

SKILLS FOCUS
All four

John Morgan

EXERCISES AROUND NUMBERS ROLE PLAY

This activity sequence is intended to produce dialogues starting with meaning rather than language. Use the idea to supplement or supplant course book dialogues.

Procedure

1 Arrange the group in a circle. Everyone numbers off round the circle.
2 Number off round the circle again. This time each person must turn to their right hand neighbour when saying their number.
3 A turns to B and says their own number. B replies to A with the next number in the series. B then turns to C and says the next number, C replies to B, then turns to D ... so on round circle.
4 Pairs: each pair holds a conversation entirely in numbers.
5 Write up on the blackboard a very limited vocabulary set, e.g., *Please, thanks, one, two, three, much, many, how, what.*
6 Tell the group that this is the total vocabulary allowed for what follows. No other words are permitted.
7 In groups of three, each group must construct a conversation (on a given theme in a given situation) using only the vocabulary on the board. (They can repeat items as often as they like and use gestures, intonation, props, etc. as they choose). The groups plan, write down, and enact the conversation for themselves.
8 Each group prepares three fair copies of their conversation and exchanges scripts with another group. They rehearse, then enact the conversations for the other group. They compare interpretations and discuss.

EXTENSION

Each individual takes a copy of the conversation they helped to write, and expands it as they like, using any vocabulary they want.

PHOTO PROXIES
Procedure

1 Ask participants to bring a personal photo (containing at least one person known to them) with them to the next day's session. About half may do so.
2 Organise the class into pairs or threes that at least one member of each group has a photo. The person with the photo answers questions from the other(s) in the role of (one of) the person(s) shown.

3.3

LEVEL
Lower intermediate +

EXTRAS
Photos of people known to your class

TIME
15 to 30 minutes

LANGUAGE FOCUS
Questions and answers

SKILLS FOCUS
Speaking and listening

John Morgan

INVISIBLE PICTURES
Procedure

1 Tell each learner to take a sheet of A4 paper, fold it in half, and imagine that it is a double page spread from their personal photo album.
2 On the paper, they then draw rectangles to represent the photos on those pages. (The rectangles may or may not represent actual photographs which the participants call to mind.) They are not to draw inside the frames.
3 In pairs, the learners describe to each other the photos.

VARIATION

This can be done as a drama exercise, with the 'photographer' using other group members as models, i.e. moulding them to portray the scenes in the 'photographs'.

RATIONALE

I find that the internal visualisation that results is a powerful aid to the talk.

3.4

LEVEL
Lower intermediate +

EXTRAS
Sheets of blank A4 paper

TIME
30 minutes

SKILLS FOCUS
Speaking and listening

John Morgan

3.5

LEVEL
Elementary +

EXTRAS
Chairs in a circle

TIME
20 minutes and up

SKILLS FOCUS
Speaking and
listening

John Morgan

THE EMPTY CHAIR (1)
Procedure

1 You and the group sit in a circle. Next to you is an empty chair. You think of someone you know well and ask the group to imagine that person filling the empty chair.
2 The group can ask the person any questions they want. You answer on that person's behalf. Questions must be direct (2nd person) and you reply in the first person. If you make a genuine attempt to empathise with the person you are answering for, and answer directly and truthfully, a mood will be set for the main activity.
3 When sufficient depth has been achieved at the first stage, rise and invite one of the group to take their place next to the empty chair; the activity continues with first one, then another group member taking on the role of someone they know. (It is advisable to 'fill the chair' with persons who are not present).
4 In subsequent sessions, or as an alternative to the second state, the group should be divided into pairs or threes, each with an empty chair to be filled by each member in turn.

VARIATIONS

a More than one empty chair may be used. I have, for example, used three empty chairs as an ice-breaking activity in groups where I wanted to establish a mood of trust quickly; I started by filling them with my wife and two sons.
b 'Empty chair' role plays can be adapted for one-to-one teaching where a common complaint is that the presence of only two persons in the group is limiting. This need not be so. Each of us is 'populated' by a host of friends, relatives, enemies, employers, employees, etc. 'Empty chair' activities can bring these vividly to life. If the teacher and learner simultaneously act for persons known to them (for example, a conversation between your mother and mine), quite complex role plays can be developed.

THE EMPTY CHAIR (2)
Procedure

1 You and the group sit in a circle. Next to you is the empty chair.
2 Ask the group to imagine an old man (or an old woman, a young boy, a soldier, etc) seated in the chair, and invite the group to give them a name.
3 One member is designated as the man's daughter/son and asked to describe their father.
4 You and other group members then ask the son/daughter questions about the old man — a picture begins to take shape.
5 After a while, you say, *X is not the only one here who knows the old man*, and invite others in the group to continue, in the role of neighbour, friend, relative, etc.

   Anyone in the group may ask anyone else questions, about the old man, about themselves (in role), or about other people in the old man's life. Gradually, even imperceptibly, a whole world is created.
6 In later sessions, sub-groups work without the teacher's intervention on their own characterisations. The activity can be used for its own sake, or as warming-up for acting out scenes.

3.6

LEVEL
Elementary +

EXTRAS
Chairs in a circle

TIME
30 minutes and up

SKILLS FOCUS
Speaking and listening

John Morgan

DOUBLING ACTIVITIES (1)

Doubling differs from conventional role playing in much the same way that 'Method' acting differs from conventional acting: Rather than construct a role, the actor attempts to become it. In many ways this is easier, one's attention is on visualising, empathising, observing the subject, rather than on technique. For this very reason, doubling is more suited to the language classroom where a learner's ability to 'act' may be more of a hindrance than a help.

Procedure

1 One member answers questions from the rest in the role of themself at a different age (earlier for older people, later for younger learners).
2 Two or more members role play a conventional situation (e.g., from the coursebook) while doubling someone known to them. This might, for example, involve a woman acting as her husband would if he were a policeman, and a man as his wife would if she were the tourist, (if the textbook role play had these two characters).
3 One member doubles one of their shoes (or their glasses, or a tooth, etc) and answers questions from the rest of the class.
4 One or more learners are directors. The rest are available as actors.

3.7

LEVEL
Upper-elementary +

EXTRAS
None

TIME
5 to 25 minutes per activity

SKILLS FOCUS
Speaking and listening

John Morgan

5 The directors each think of a situation from their own experience involving themselves and one or more other people.

6 The directors decide the characters and the casting, not forgetting to choose someone to take on their role since they themselves are busy directing.

7 The directors go off with their actors and teach them how to play the scene. Any members not needed as actors are free to move around and listen in to the work of the different sub-groups. There should be no performance afterwards in front of the whole group since this would lend a feeling of rehearsal to this, the really important stage of the activity.

3.8

LEVEL
Intermediate +

EXTRAS
None

TIME
45 to 90 minutes

SKILLS FOCUS
Speaking and listening

John Morgan

DOUBLING ACTIVITIES (2)

Johnson's biographer James Boswell wrote that he was acutely aware that he had a London self and a Scottish self; many of us may feel similar divisions. Doubling provides an opportunity to express and exploit this richness.

Procedure

DIVIDED SELF

1 One member of the group volunteers to be the protagonist and sits where everyone can see them.

2 The protagonist tells the group of an aspect of character in which they feel divided – e.g., between tolerance and authoritarianism – and chooses two members to represent these sides of them.

3 The 'alter egos' sit one on each side of the protagonist, but a little behind. The rest of the group now put questions to the protagonist, which are answered by each of the alter egos in role, that is, in the first person. The protagonist is silent throughout.

4 After 5 to 10 questions have been asked and answered, the protagonist may comment on the answers given.

MORAL TRIANGLES

1 The group is divided into threes. Each trio sits in a triangle as above. That is, A and B sit on each side of, and a little behind, C, all facing the same way. A is the 'tough' side C, and B the 'soft' side (or any similar opposition).

2 You (or another group member) then read out a short description of a moral problem. This should be written in the second person, i.e., directly addressed to C. An example might begin, 'You are a UN aid worker in a famine area. One day a consignment of grain arrives. You

begin to distribute the grain, but soon discover that the local lorry-owners will only let you use their lorries if you let them have a large proportion of the grain to sell on the black market . . .'.

3 After the reading, in each trio, A and B simultaneously whisper their solutions to the problem to C. After one or two minutes they stop, and C gives them his/her response.

(I learnt this from a workshop given by Richard Baudains)

COMMENTS

Central to all the photo, empty chair and doubling role plays is the factor of empathy with real people rather than (stereo)typical roles. The deepest level of role play will involve those actually present in the group. (Whether a given group should or is prepared to undertake this will be a matter for some judgement).

Many familiar classroom activities can be developed to achieve empathetic communication. Here is one example:

1 A common 'information gap' activity goes like this:

  a The group pairs off and you give each learner a drawing or magazine picture, which they may look at but must keep secret from their partner.

  b By questioning, the partner attempts to discover as much as possible about the picture, and then either draws or describes it.

  c The first development of the activity is to remove the pictures, each partner is asked to construct the image mentally.

  d By questioning, their partner has to find out and reconstruct it. The attention of each is focused on the other, rather than on the material.

  e The second, empathetic development is to include the partner in the mental picture. Each participant looks at their partner and imagines them in a setting. In both the construction and reconstruction of the mental picture, the participants focus not only on each other but on their mutual perception.

2 Instead of immediately starting a discussion on some theme of current interest, participants list, without expressing any personal commitment, the possible points of view, attitudes, etc., that might be taken, and think of real people who might have such commitments. Then (and only then) they hold the discussion – each member speaking on behalf of one of these people.

Recommended reading on role plays:

Blatner A 1973 *Acting In: Practical Applications of Psychodramatic Method* Springer N.Y.

Dufeu B and Feldhendler D Various articles in 'Le Francais dans le monde' (Avril 1983) (jeu de role, psychodrama and 'psychodramaturgie linguistique')

Leverton, E 1977 *Psychodrama for the Timid Clinician* ***Springer N.Y.***

Miller, K 1985 *Doubles* OUP (on the divided self theme in literature

Moreno, JL 1975 *Psychodrama* (2 volumes) Beacon House

Moreno, JL 1975 *Psychotherapie de groupe et psychodrame* Retz (Les classiques des sciences humaines)

Saretsky, T 1977 *Active Techniques and Group Therapy* Jason Aronson

Morgan, J and Rinvolucri M, 1988 *The Q Book* Longman (contains a number of role play questioning activities)

Acknowledgements to Mario Rinvolucri, Bernard Dufeu and Richard Baudains for many of the ideas expressed in the empty chair and doubling role plays.

CHAPTER 4

Using visuals

Visuals remain, in the vast majority of classrooms, wildly under-exploited. We hope the activities in this chapter (as well as those in our companion volume, David A. Hill's *Visual Impact*) may entice you into broadening your exploitation of the fantastic abundance of visual materials, especially magazine pictures, which surrounds all but the most remotely situated teachers.

FUZZY XEROX

Before undertaking the exercise suggested here it is important to establish whether or not the picture is in copyright as it is illegal to make multiple copies of any material which is in copyright.

Procedure

1 Copy and recopy a picture until the lines become indistinct. The result should be evocative and patterned, but should not give too strong clues as to the original picture. (You may need to experiment with the photocopier to achieve this. Try varying the contrast, magnification, and distance of the original from the glass).
2 Give out one copy of the fuzzy xerox to each learner. Ask the group to make sense of the picture and to draw in (preferably in black felt tip pen) the main outlines of what they see.
3 You can continue in various ways:
   a Ask members to mill around and explain their pictures to one another.
   b Ask them to jot down six to ten words suggested by the picture they have produced, and then to include these words in a paragraph about their picture or some image brought to mind by it. When they have finished their paragraphs, they should write only their six to ten key words on a blank page but in exactly the same position as they appear on the sheet of paper bearing their paragraph.
   Each learner gives their very 'gapped' text, with the picture, to another member of the group for completion. The pairs then compare texts.
   c Ask members to attach their pictures to the wall to form an exhibition. In turn, each then gives a two-minute talk to the rest about their picture, the artist, setting, technique, etc.

4.1

LEVEL
Intermediate +

EXTRAS
A blurred photocopy of a picture, black felt tip pens

TIME
30 to 60 minutes

SKILLS FOCUS
All four

John Morgan

4.2

LEVEL
Elementary +

EXTRAS
Dozens of pictures
and one story

TIME
15 to 30 minutes

SKILLS FOCUS
Speaking and
listening

John Morgan

PICTURE SPREAD
Procedure

1 Tell the group a story.
2 Then spread out a large number of pictures (at least 100 for a group of 15) and ask everyone to choose one picture each that for them represents or reminds them of an important theme/aspect of the story. Both story and pictures should be rich and ambiguous. Do *not* select pictures for the story. Let the learners work from a variety.
3 Learners talk about their picture in pairs or groups.

VARIATION

You can use this activity as a follow on from a silent reading as well.

EDITOR'S NOTE

The magazines that come with Sunday newspapers are a fantastic source of pictures. It takes no time at all to amass a substantial collection.

4.3

LEVEL
Lower
intermediate +

EXTRAS
Pictures and
cartoons

TIME
30 to 40 minutes

SKILLS FOCUS
Writing and reading

John Morgan

ILLUSTRATING NEWSPAPERS
Procedure

1 Spread out a large collection of pictures, cartoons, etc.
2 Ask learners to select one picture from the collection that interests, intrigues or disturbs them.
3 Remove all pictures that remain after this.
4 Ask members to imagine that their picture is an illustration to a magazine or newspaper article. Tell them to draft the article in their head, not to write anything down.
5 When they have a clear idea of their article, they should write a short (one or two paragraphs) letter to the magazine editor agreeing or disagreeing with the article (which is still only in their minds).
6 Collect the resulting letters and display them for group reading. They can, as well, provide a starting point for deeper exploration of the themes that emerge.

THEME RANKING
Procedure

4.4

LEVEL
Lower intermediate +

EXTRAS
Identical sets of 10 to 20 pictures

TIME
45 to 60 minutes

SKILLS FOCUS
Speaking and listening

John Morgan

Prepare sets of 10 to 20 pictures for each group of 8 to 12 members. Each picture should occupy no more than half of its A4 sheet, leaving the rest of the space free for writing.

1 The pictures are circulated round each group.
2 Each learner is allowed to write up to three words on each picture to express what they consider to be the main themes of the picture.
3 When all the pictures have been dealt with, the group looks at all pictures and themes and chooses the ten most important or interesting themes and ranks them in order of priority.
4 Each group explains their ranking and the reasoning behind it to the whole class. The result is, in fact, a group discussion of a number of things that interest them.

This is an excellent way of establishing a course agenda.

DIARIES
Procedure

4.5

LEVEL
Elementary +

EXTRAS
Pictures you do not wish to use again

TIME
30 to 45 minutes

SKILLS FOCUS
Writing and reading

John Morgan

1 On a large table or on the floor, spread out a collection of pictures (fuzzy or clear) that do not contain any human figures.
2 Ask everyone to choose one each, and then to add a human being somewhere.
3 When they have done this, everyone should imagine:
   a a date for the picture
   b the place
   c a name and skeleton biography for the person they added
4 They should then compose a diary entry of 100–200 words to recount that moment in their lives.
5 Display the pictures and diary entries along the walls or on table or desk tops.

4.6

LEVEL
Advanced

EXTRAS
One copy for each learner of an 'A Day in the Life of X' article. These are in most colour supplement magazines.

TIME
70 to 90 minutes

LANGUAGE FOCUS
Lexis for times of the day, vocabulary in general

SKILLS FOCUS
Reading, speaking, listening, and writing

Tessa Woodward

A DAY IN THE LIFE

The photo and text should be cut out separately and pasted on card.

Procedure

1 Draw on the board some symbols at the top of columns, as shown in Fig. 7

Fig. 7

2 Put up one example in each column of a related time phrase used to refer to a part of a day, (see Fig. 8).

| at sunrise | after dark | in the coffee break | before I go to work | about 6-ish |

Fig. 8

3 Learners brainstorm individually and in pairs all the time phrases they can think of. Then you add some more. You can get over 50 quite easily, e.g. *at dawn, at sunrise at twilight, at dusk, in the small hours, at elevenses, in the lunch hour, in the rush-hour*, etc.

4 Tell the learners about the 'A Day in the Life' series. They predict what tenses (don't stop at one!) could come up in such a text and why.

5 Each learner gets a different text. Learners read once for pleasure, then again noting down any phrases they would like to use in the re-telling.

6 Learners pair up and tell each other about their person without looking at the text. The aim is for each to give their partner a feeling for the personality behind the text.

7 After both learners have spoken, they imagine together what their people would wear and would look like.

8 Meanwhile, you have been pinning up the photos around the room, spaced far apart and away from the learners' view. (Be sure you've eliminated all obvious name clues from text and photo-caption).

9 The learners then walk about and try to find the photo of their person.

10 Learners discuss if their person looked as they imagined they would.

11 Working with the texts, learners pull out phrases they would like to use when writing their own 'Day in the Life' for homework.

I learnt the idea of separating pictures from texts from a teacher at South Devon Technical College some years ago. I've forgotten his name, sorry!

CHAPTER 5

Vocabulary: systems for word learning

The activities in this chapter all concern learning vocabulary. Of course, each brings various other skills into play as well, listening, speaking, reading, or extended writing. But though the theme and range of skills involved may differ from activity to activity, in every case there is an emphasis on equipping learners with strategies and techniques which they can apply in learning new words and phrases in general.

5.1

LEVEL
Elementary +

EXTRAS
Good quality
white or blackboard

TIME
45 to 60 minutes

SKILLS FOCUS
How words are
organised into word
families

***Seth
Lindstromberg***

SORTING AND STEPPING

This is an activity for refining learners' understanding of how words are organised into meaning families, for refining their understanding of words they already know, for reviewing and practising these words, for teaching a few new words that are related in meaning to the ones already known and for leaving learners with easy to comprehend diagrammatic 'definitions' to which example sentences can be added.

Procedure

1 On a black or whiteboard write six to twelve words from between two and four small lexical families all jumbled up on the board. Allow no note taking yet! In an elementary class your boardwork might look like this:

surprising   terrifying   exciting   interesting
fascinating   thrilling   frightening   astonishing

Fig. 9

Some words for intermediates, similarly jumbled, could be: *huge, teeny-weeny, enormous, big, vast, little, tiny* ...

Ones for advanced learners, again jumbled, could be, for example: *perplexed, baffled, affected, overwhelmed, dismayed, appalled, put off, disgusted, revolted, nauseated, impressed, awestruck* ...

2 Let's take the last group of words as an example. Invite learners to go to the board and circle the words they think they know.

3 Taking the circled words one-by-one, point to each and ask if there are any other circled words that mean roughly the same as it does.

4 When a learner gives a correct 'relative', draw a line connecting the two circles. Continue until the learners have run out of ideas. Then carry on yourself to link up the various related words.

You may want to use different colours of marker or chalk for connecting up words in different mini-families or make the lines between members of one family solid, between members of another wiggly, and so on.

5 For each mini-group of 'synonyms', (eg *perplexed* and *baffled*), ask which is the most general, least intense word. If given a wrong answer, demur and say everything will be clear in a bit. Still no note taking!

6 When you've elicited all the connections you can get, tell learners to take a last look because you're going to test them! Give them about 20 seconds and then erase everything.

7 Ask learners to tell you one of the vanished words which they knew the meaning of. If someone says '*Appalled*', ask what word went with it. You virtually always get the right answer from someone.

8 Check again which is the least intense. If no one knows, now is the time to reveal all. Say they can take notes now.

9 Write this on the board:

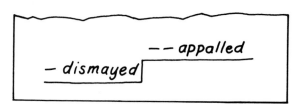

Fig. 10

10 Invite people to come forward and draw stairstep diagrams for the other families. Elicit plus and minus signs, or other symbols, to indicate connotation. Add the diagrams that no one else can do.

11 For each word, ask for things, events, experiences or situations that cause someone to feel that way. Start with the mini-families that learners seem to know best. Thus, you might be impressed that someone could speak five languages well, but are awestruck to discover one day that they could speak twenty-five perfectly.

Once learners get the idea, they're quite good at making appropriate contexts for a word they didn't know before, after they see it linked to one they did know.

NOTE

Sometimes you can make quite long stairsteps (as for the words given for intermediates). Sometimes you'll want to put two or more words on the same level (e.g. *puzzled, perplexed*).

If no word in a mini-family is known, some teaching is called for. But try to avoid this by concentrating on families at least one member of which you're pretty sure your learners will know.

VARIATIONS

a With some sorts of words, you'll proceed a bit differently. With words like *borrow, lend, buy, sell, offer* ..., you'd ask which of the other words were more like *give* and which were more like *take*. The aim would be to make two columns along that principle.

b Some word families are best displayed by a kind of diagram I call a 'hydra' where the more specific descriptive verbs (e.g. *stroll*) are grouped around the basic verb (in this case, *walk*) and connected to it by lines. Adrian Underhill's *Use Your Dictionary* (1980, Oxford University Press) contains several interesting examples.

RATIONALE

The aim of this activity is not so much to teach vocabulary as to educate learners in ways of thinking about words and ways of succinctly recording what they know about their family relationships. My experience is that learners take to drawing diagrams like ducks to water.

5.2

LEVEL
Advanced

EXTRAS
Optional:
thesauruses and
dictionaries

TIME
60 to 90 minutes

LANGUAGE FOCUS
Vocabulary for
expressing emotions

SKILLS FOCUS
Speaking, listening,
note taking

Tessa Woodward

EXPRESSING EMOTIONS

Procedure

PHASE ONE: ADJECTIVES

1 Introduce learners, via the board, to the idea of plotting adjectives along a scale, e.g.,

| freezing | cold | chilly | cold | warm | hot | boiling |

2 Add as many related words to this scale as possible.

3 Brainstorm some emotions, e.g. *happiness, sadness, anger, surprise, disappointment, love,* etc.

4 Learners in twos or threes choose one emotion and brainstorm all the adjectives they can think of to express shades or aspects of it, e.g. *happiness: elated, joyful, light-hearted, cheerful, ecstatic.*

5 Return to plenary again. Each pair or trio reads out their collection. The others listen and add any new adjectives they can think of. For example, if the 'happiness' pair reads out the words given in point 4, other learners might add *on top of the world* or *content.*

6 The learners return to work in the same twos or threes. Ask them to sort out their pool of words onto a scale. They may consult you, other pairs or trios or use a dictionary, thesaurus, or the *Longman Lexicon of Contemporary English* (McArthur, 1981).

PHASE TWO: PHRASES

7 Next, ask learners to imagine they're chatting to someone who is feeling the emotion they have chosen, or that this someone is telling an anecdote about a time when they felt that emotion.

8 Ask them to brainstorm all the phrases the person might use. For example, the 'love' group might come up with: *I was quite fond of him, I was head over heels in love, Absolutely besotted, We got on quite well.*

9 Briefly return to plenary so that the groups can read out their phrases and the other groups can suggest additions.

10 Next, ask learners to rank these phrases by strength of emotion. (This idea I got from Gerlinde Wilberg who learnt it on a marriage guidance counselling course).

PHASE THREE: WRITTEN TEXT

11 Take any text written in a strong, definite style. For fun, a page out of a melodramatic Mills and Boon best-seller.

12 Learners underline or circle any verb which is very emotionally descriptive.

13 Ask them to translate the text into a bland, more general vocabulary. Thus, 'he gripped her hands' becomes 'he held her hands'.

14 Lead a general discussion on how fine choice of adjective, phrase, or verb can lead to schmaltz, sentimentality or good range of expressiveness. Use your learners' own examples.

RATIONALE

Inexperienced teachers often misjudge upper intermediate learners as advanced (learner fluency is noticed, but weaknesses are not). One result is that these teachers tend to swamp their upper-intermediates with tasks that are too difficult. These mistakes are not too difficult to grow out of though. In the long run, true advanced classes present an even greater challenge, even to the experienced teacher. One is bound to wonder, sometimes, what is left to teach them. Fortunately – for a teacher in this state of mind – advanced learners are generally extremely keen on learning new vocabulary and, especially, set phrases. Giving a vocabulary lesson too narrow a focus is risky. Some learners are bound to know a lot of the lexis you have in mind to teach and will be disappointed at learning nothing new. A direction for teaching advanced classes lies in the fact that they are what they know usually very mixed in level. That is, each probably knows a great deal of lexis that none of the others do. Use them to teach each other and they can all learn lots of new words, and keep talking more actively too.

5.3

LEVEL
Upper intermediate

EXTRAS
Newspaper or
magazine articles

TIME
20 minutes per
article/text

**LANGUAGE
FOCUS**
Vocabulary in
categories

SKILLS FOCUS
All four

Mario Rinvolucri

WHOLE BODY IMAGES

Procedure

1 Give out a passage, such as the one in Fig. 11, for the learners to read through for gist. Perhaps divide the article into quarters and give a time limit per quarter, to keep people from reading too, carefully.

2 Ask your learners to turn their papers over and rule three columns on a sheet of paper. The column headings are:

Eye Words   Ear Words   Whole Body Words

3 Tell them you will read the article to them slowly. They are to note down visual words, images and phrases in the first column and auditory ones in the second column. The third column is for words and phrases that represent ideas through whole body imagery.

4 Read the passage slowly while they take down those words and phrases.

5 They compare their personal categorisation of the words with their neighbour's.

6 Hold a general discussion.

NOTE

This bit of advertising in Fig. 11 is remarkable for its whole body imagery, but similar texts are not too difficult to find.

ACKNOWLEDGEMENT

The above ideas derive from the work of Bandler and Grinder (see for example, *Frogs into Princes*, Bandler and Grinder 1974).

WHIZZZ!!!
See what happens when you let go of the dead man's handle.

CLUNK
Operate the points in a life size section of tube tunnel.

Find out how to set off the emergency warning on a modern bus.

CLIPP CLOPP!
Take yourself back to the age of the horse drawn bus.

PURRR
Enter the silent world of trolleybuses.

HONN-KK!
Work the controls of a real double-decker bus.

Ph-ut-tt!!
Discover some of London's earliest motor buses.

HISSSS!
See how the safety systems work on the underground.

It doesn't sound like a museum, does it?

As you can see, at the London Transport Museum, the emphasis is very much on activity and involvement.

You'll find it's a far cry from the hushed reverence of some of London's more established museums.

And, in our opinion, all the better for it.

If it all sounds like fun, it's meant to be. But it's also a highly effective way of stimulating interest in how people's lives have been affected by the growth of transport systems in London.

For more information on educational activities and group visits please write or phone: London Transport Museum, The Piazza, Covent Garden, London WC2E 7BB.
Tel: 01-379 6344.

Fig. 11

5.4

LEVEL
Upper intermediate

EXTRAS
Bilingual or
monolingual
dictionaries

TIME
30 minutes

SKILLS FOCUS
listening, note taking,
reading, speaking

Mario Rinvolucri

LEARNING-PROCESS STORIES

Procedure

1 Read the passage to the learners and ask them as they listen to jot down all the words they hear that are connected with mathematics.

Decimals flummox maths pupils

'A large proportion of pupils in secondary schools do not understand a concept which is the cornerstone of our number system. They are confused by 'place value', the idea that the value of a digit depends on the column in which it is placed. This conclusion has been reached by the Assessment of Performance Unit (APU), which last week published the results of tests on 11 and 15 year olds over the period 1978–1982.

The difficulty children have appears clearly when they are asked to write a fraction, such as 4/100, as a decimal. Only 38 per cent of 11 year olds got this right and the success rate had only risen to 53 per cent at age 15. An alarming number of 11 year olds – nearly one in five – opted for the answer 4.100. By 15, only a few per cent of children make this mistake.

The test asked pupils to write a series of decimals in ascending or descending order. Four out of five 11 year olds were completely flummoxed. Even at 15, around half of children could not put the numbers in the right order.

The report finds, however, that if decimal computations are placed in simple, everyday contexts, children do better. If pupils aged 11 are asked to calculate 13/2, only 28 per cent will get it right. But, if instead they are told that a chocolate bar 13 centimetres long is cut in half, then asked, 'How long will each piece be?', the success rate leaps to 81 per cent.

According to the authors of the study, 'The most helpful context for 11 year olds appears to be money'. The reason seems to be that children then have the option of translating a problem involving decimal fractions, which they find difficult to handle, into a problem involving whole numbers, which they are much happier dealing with. Pupils convert everything into pence before manipulating the numbers.

The oddest thing is that children cannot generalise this process. Although they have a method for dealing with pounds and pence, or metres and centimetres, they cannot abstract this to units and hundredths, for instance. The authors say that 'links between the decimal system and various metric systems of measurement are not seen by many pupils'.

Decimals: Assessment at Age 11 and 15, NFER-NELSON, Darville House, 2 Oxford Road East, Windsor, SL4 1DF *New Scientist* 10 July, 1986

2 Ask the learners to compare the words they have taken down.
3 They read the passage and check out hard words in their dictionaries.

4 Ask them to jot down the names of all the mathematics teachers they have had.

5 Tell the group the story of your relationship with mathematics as a learning process.

6 Put them in groups of three or four and invite them to tell each other their mathematics stories.

NOTE ON LEVEL

The only thing that makes this an upper intermediate exercise is the language level of the passage above. If you chop the hard bits out, you can do the exercise at much lower levels. And clearly, there are aspects of this activity that can be applied to many other texts as well.

REAL RESEARCH: MIXING ADVANCED LEARNERS WITH TRAINEE TEACHERS

5.5

LEVEL
Advanced

EXTRAS
None

TIME
90 minutes

LANGUAGE FOCUS
Vocabulary (for the learners)

SKILLS FOCUS
Speaking, listening, and note taking

Seth Lindstromberg

If your school runs courses both for advanced learners of English and for novice or would-be native speaking teachers of English, here's an idea you can use to add to the amount of contact your learners have with native speakers.

1 Prepare the advanced learners to interview the native speakers by setting them the task of noting down any expression the native speaker uses which is unfamiliar to them or which, while not unfamiliar, is not part of their active vocabulary but they would like it to be. Give them five minutes to prepare questions in groups, but do not encourage people all to ask the same questions.

2 The native speakers are, meanwhile given the task of looking to see what the learners have noted down and noting it down in turn. This they are to do as the interview is ending, not as the learners make their jottings.

3 When the two groups meet, establish a rota so that each learner or pair of learners interviews at least three trainees for seven to ten minutes each.

4 As each interview period ends, call time and make sure the native speakers all move one position along to the next interviewer(s).

5 After the interviews, bring the learners together and get them to report the expressions they have collected. They invariably have got something of interest. Write these on the board, categorising them as you go. Or ask one of your class to take the role of teacher. (If it's an advanced class, you've probably got some English teachers anyway.) Or, the learners form groups of four or so, pool their expressions themselves and write them onto posters which they hang along the walls. Or they write their expressions on A4 sheets which are then photocopied and distributed.

6 Meanwhile, the native speakers are doing something very similar, but with special emphasis on categorising the learners' notes (e.g. as idioms, faddish terms, dialect terms, etc.).

RATIONALE

For the learners:
It's absurd for fifteen learners to be sitting in a room with one teacher when down the corridor there are twelve would-be teachers wondering what it's going to be like when they have their own class, maybe their own advanced class. If native speakers are language resources, one per fifteen learners is obviously not the optimum ratio.

Perhaps this activity can be the beginning of the development of a self-led learning strategy which the learners can continue to apply for the rest of the course with host families (if they are in an English speaking country) or other native speakers. That is, they can continue to collect expressions for pooling with classmates.

For the native speakers:
Novice teachers rarely have any conception of what advanced learners (or even upper intermediate learners) need or want to learn; they have little or no sense of where these learners have gaps in their knowledge of English. This is what this activity can help them begin to learn. It might also interest them to hear of self-led language learning.

This idea evolved during a language improvement course for foreign teachers of English at Pilgrims in 1987. I think the idea began either with Tessa Woodward or Mario Rinvolucri. Certainly Mario was the main force behind mixing our native speaking introductory training course people with learners in general.

FAVOURITE WORDS ORGY

Each learner unconsciously (or consciously) has favourite words. Maybe they like the sound or the meaning or the context or the spelling ... there are lots of reasons for preferring one word to another. The aim of this activity is to foster an awareness of such preferences in your learners.

Procedure

1 The activity can begin with you saying something like this, *My favourite word is 'pudding'. English people try to be so refined when they are in restaurants. 'What is the dessert?' But at home they say 'What's for pudding?'. And it sounds dense and sweet and very filling — 'pu ... pud ... pudd ... pudding'. And imagine it as a verb pud, 'Are you pudding? Have you pudded?'*

2 Ask learners to think of one or two favourite words and spend a bit of time wondering why they are so likeable.

3 Then, ask learners what their favourite words are and write them on the board. Find out what people like about their words.

4 Explore with the group any similarities among words.

5 Get the whole class to read the words aloud together. Experiment with special voices or tones for different words. Don't neglect to do some lively work on the basics of pronunciation and make sure everyone knows what the favourite words mean.

6 Everyone stands up and moves around shaking hands with everyone else. Use your favourite word (or someone else's!) as a greeting. Do this very briskly.

7 Then ask learners in pairs to find new words that fit well with the words on the board and to make up a dialogue including three or four of the words on the board and three or four further words that fit well with them.

8 When the first two pairs are ready, invite them to perform their dialogues for each other. Keep pairing off pairs like this. If the first pairs finish their performances quickly, recycle each pair by sending them off to perform their dialogues for someone else. This phase continues until each pair have performed their dialogue at least once.

EXTENSIONS

1 Learners poll a set number of native speakers of English about their favourite words, what they mean, how they use them, and why they like them.

2 They share the results of their polls in the following class, perhaps by making posters to display what they learned.

3 As a warm-up to a later lesson, learners sit in groups as if at a gourmet meal and share favourite words like delicacies. (Mime is important here.) At higher levels, the words are woven into conversation as well.

5.6

LEVEL
Beginner +

EXTRAS
Large black/whiteboard

TIME
60 to 90 minutes

SKILLS FOCUS
Speaking and listening

AIM
To activate learners' esthetic feelings for English words.

Jim Wingate

VARIATIONS

1 Learners present their favourite words in their own language to the whole group and lead the other learners in saying them.
2 Everyone tries to think of the English equivalents. (Bilingual dictionaries might come in handy.)
3 The group discusses the aesthetic merits of the various mother tongue and English 'twins'.
4 Learners use English words that they judge likeable in favourite word dialogues as above.

Mario Rinvolucri and John Morgan first introduced me to the idea of using favourite words.

5.7

LEVEL
Elementary +

EXTRAS
At least one thesaurus

TIME
40 to 60 minutes

SKILLS FOCUS
Speaking and listening

Jim Wingate

HATED WORDS VENGEANCE

Do this after *Favourite Words Orgy*.

Procedure

1 Start out something like this: *There are some words you dislike. I dislike ...* (Write some words you dislike on the board.)
2 Invite learners to say what words they dislike and write them up on the board.
3 Everyone says these aloud with hatred and venom. If the energy is high, shout the words all together.
4 Elicit a few more words, if necessary and then ask everyone to have an argument with a neighbour first of all using only these words (with no connecting words), then, after one or two arguments, ask learners to change partners and have arguments using the words connected into sentences.
5 Now have five minutes of discussing why the various words are so dislikeable, that is, what they bring to mind and so forth. At lower levels, this is an opportunity to feed in such language as,
... makes me feel (like) ... reminds me of ....
6 Then, everyone searches for new words (perhaps using a thesaurus or the *Longman Lexicon*) which might replace those words and be likeable or at least neutral.
7 Collect these on the board.
8 Then all search for words which might be even more hateable for the same things.
9 Collect those on the board.
10 Practise and discuss the sounds and rhythm.

EXTENSION FOR INTERMEDIATE CLASSES

Finally, pairs, using the words accumulated on the board, create a political speech in two versions, one using the hated words, the other using bland versions of them. Each then delivers a version of the speech to the class.

VERBAL DYNAMICS

Here is an activity that combines word and action, word and observation, and the use of words in a learner-created context to make new language especially memorable.

Procedure

1 Choose six to eight verbs that you want to practise. They may be words from a text you are using or they may be words that you have especially chosen to practise a pronunciation point. The words you choose must be 'doing' words.

For a young class you may have words like *hop, jump, run, skip, swim, climb, smile,* and *frown.*

For an older, more advanced class, words like these have worked well: *throttle, threaten, throng, thread, thieve, thrill,* and *throb.*
2 Memorise the words.
3 Everyone stands in a circle, including you.
4 Begin by saying one of the words. Ask if anyone knows what it means. If someone does, ask them to do it, that is, to mime it. If no one knows, you mime and the learners copy.
5 Work through all of the words in this way.
6 Go through them all quickly a second time.
7 Ask someone who remembers some of the words to call them out. As the words are called out, everyone mimes the actions again. If the caller dries up, ask someone else to continue. Keep going until most people can remember most of the words.
8 Divide the class into groups. The exact size of the group is not important.
9 Ask each group to try to recall the words and then choose about five of them to work into a mimed scene.
10 Each group then mimes their story for the others.
11 As they watch, the spectators should call out any of the original words as they 'happen'.
12 The learners then talk about what they observed and see if it tallies with what the group intended.

5.8

LEVEL
Elementary to intermediate

TIME
15 minutes. Up to an hour with the extension

EXTRAS
None

SKILLS FOCUS
Speaking; listening; writing

Judy Baker

EXTENSION

The learners write the scenario for the mime-story they liked the most.

ACKNOWLEDGEMENT

I first learnt this type of exercise from Eve Ogonowski, but I believe the idea and the title come from *Into the Life of Things: An Exploration of Language through Verbal Dynamics* (Burniston 1972).

5.9

LEVEL
Elementary to intermediate

TIME
15 minutes as a warm-up or filler; longer if main activity.

EXTRAS
A pack of playing cards or slips of paper with words written on them

LANGUAGE FOCUS
Practice revision of vocabulary

Bryan Robinson

LEXIS POKER

PREPARATION

Collect vocabulary items that your class have met recently. You can get your class to help you with this by asking them, the day before, to make short lists of items they'd like to learn but are afraid they won't or of items particular people in the class ought to learn but probably won't. (It can be fun if learners note down the person who ought to learn each word. This information can be shared after the poker game.)

Allot each player an equal number of poker chips, matches, or play money. These may be given out free, or someone (probably you) takes on the role of banker by selling the chips (or whatever) or making change.

Organise the class into groups of players, with no more than six per group. Each group sits at a separate table. First, however, you will need to demonstrate the rules by playing with one small group while the rest of the class stands around.

Procedure

1 Each player puts an agreed sum of tokens, or money, into the centre of the table. This is the 'ante'.
2 The dealer deals each player three cards.
3 The players look at their cards and silently try to produce one of the following:
    a One sentence using all three of the vocabulary items involved.
    b Two sentences, with two of the items in one sentence and the other in the second sentence.
4 Players who decide that they cannot complete this task, may ante again and take one additional card, so can players who can use all their words in one or two sentences but who think that they could also do the more ambitious task in step 5. Anyone who thinks they have a terrible set of words and does not want to risk more money may give up, that is, they may 'stack' or 'fold' their cards.

5 When all players who wish to have drawn a fourth card, ask them to form, silently, one of the following:

   a One sentence using all four items.

   b Two sentences, which use up all four of the items.

6 Again, players decide whether to stack or stay in the game with the cards that they have (i.e. to 'hold') or to buy an additional card, that is, to try for a better hand (i.e. set of cards) by risking more tokens or money.

7 Now, some players may have five cards (the maximum) while others have four or even only three, depending on whether and how often they held. Others may be out of the hand (i.e. this game). It is time for the players to begin betting. (Set a limit on the amount of money or tokens per bet.)

8 The player to the dealer's left has the first opportunity to bet. If they decline to bet (i.e. if they 'check'), the turn passes clockwise. If some-one bets, that is, puts a sum of money or of tokens that they wish to risk into the middle of the table, then every player following them must either bet the same amount (i.e. 'call') or stack or 'raise'. If they raise, they bet more than the amount of the previous bet. This new, additional sum must be put into the middle of the table by everyone who has already bet. Anyone who hasn't already bet must put in the sum of the original bet plus the sum of the raise. (Set a limit on the number of raises, say two or three.)

Learners bet according to how good they think their sentence/s is/are. Or, if they think they can frighten other players out of the game, they may 'bluff', that is, bet as though they have a good hand even though they haven't.

9 When everyone has either called all the bets or has stacked, the players still in the game read out their sentences. The best ones take the 'pot' (i.e. the tokens or money in the middle of the table). If there is a draw, the money stays in the 'kitty' (i.e. the middle of the table) for the next hand, which all players may join again. The order of pre-cedence of hands, from best to worst is:

5 items in one sentence
4 items in one sentence plus 1 in another
4 items in one sentence
3 items in one sentence plus 2 in another
3 items in one sentence plus 1 in another
3 items in one sentence
2 items in one sentence and 2 in another
2 items in one sentence and 1 in another

CHAPTER 6

Free speech and other skills

This chapter consists mostly of activities which can get your learners using English to express thoughts that matter to them. One or two focus a bit more on accuracy . . . or on fun. Some of the activities call for writing, all call for speaking.

6.1

LEVEL
Intermediate +

EXTRAS
Cards with adverbs to be practised

TIME
10 to 20 minutes

LANGUAGE FOCUS
Adverbs

Paulina Ludlow-Brown

HEDGES

Introduce this idea to intermediate/advanced groups in order to help them overcome long hesitations and excessive *umming and aahing*, hopefully enabling them to cover up their loss of words.

Make small cards bearing the target adverbs (i.e. *well, actually, really, frankly, etc*) and other similar ones. A dozen or so will do.

Procedure

1 Deal four or five cards to each learner.
2 The learners must use one of their words before each sentence.
3 As each learner says their word/phrase, they discard that card.
4 Otherwise, people try to have a normal conversation about a topic of their choice.
5 The discussion continues until everyone has used up all their cards.

VARIATIONS

a Learners can use the words on their cards when and where they like in the discussion.
b You flourish a red card in case of incorrect use of a word. When you do this, the person who made the mistake must retrieve their card.
c If someone manages to use a word so naturally that no one notices them putting their card down, they get a prize! (This idea is Tessa Woodward's.)

JIGSAW DOING: USING A NATURE TRAIL

For this idea to work you have to have a trail, country walk, or scenic urban walk nearby which can be divided into clear sections and for which there exists a map, though you can always draw up a map yourself.

Procedure

1 Photocopy the map and chop it up into sections so that each pair or trio of learners has a section each. Help the learners to interpret the map, that is, say what they'd expect to see on their part of the walk.
2 The learners then go out on their part of the walk with pen and paper and plastic bags.
3 They write notes on anything they notice and like or find interesting and bring back in the plastic bag something that is special to their part of the walk and, probably, no other part.
4 Back in the classroom learners produce posters with an enlarged picture of their route on it and pictures and notes giving extra information. Grasses, flowers, feathers, etc. can be stuck on the map. You can circulate, helping with language problems. You may need a book on trees and flowers to help with classification.
5 All the posters are displayed and learners tell each other about their part of the trail.
6 Together the class builds up a picture of the whole walk. You can then go and do the whole walk together if you want.

6.2

LEVEL
Elementary +

EXTRAS
A map of a nature trail; a book on flora; paper

TIME
90 to 120 minutes. Can be done over two lessons

LANGUAGE FOCUS
Vocabulary

SKILLS FOCUS
Speaking and listening

REQUIREMENT
Going outside

Tessa Woodward

6.3

LEVEL
Elementary +

EXTRAS
One dice per group of four players

TIME
30 minutes (imagination), 50 minutes (reality)

LANGUAGE FOCUS
Exponents of suggestion

SKILLS FOCUS
Speaking and listening

Jean-Paul Creton

THE DICEMASTER

This activity can be played at two levels: the purely imaginative in class and in reality within a given environment.

Procedure

In the imagination:
1 Each group has a leader, 'The Dicemaster', whose function is to record the options and roll the dice.
2 You or the class decide what theme to explore, e.g. 'holidays', 'school', 'marriage', 'next weekend', etc.
3 Each group then create five options related to the topic, and give each one a number on the dice. The sixth option must be: 'The Dicemaster dies', which acts as a cut-off point for the activity.
4 The Dicemaster rolls the dice and according to whichever option comes up, learners must create five more options from that situation. For example, 'holidays' might lead to 'visit Spain' to 'fight a bull' to 'end up in hospital' to 'fall in love with a Spanish doctor' and so on.
5 If 'The Dicemaster dies' turns up, that group is out of the game and may disperse to observe other groups. The winning group is the one still playing when chance has eliminated all the other groups.

In reality:
Each group has a Dicemaster, as before, however, the sixth option is always 'appoint a new Dicemaster'. When this comes up, all previous options must be cancelled and a new Dicemaster takes over.
1 Each individual group decides on five options which are feasible within the environment set by you. The only other limit is that a time is set for all players to be back in class. Otherwise players must follow the dictates of chance according to the options which turn up.
2 In the event that a group 'chicken out' on an option they have set themselves, they must return to class and confess their failure.
3 Learners must be back in class at the time set by you, the Dice Lord, in order to report their journey and adventures.

ACKNOWLEDGEMENT

I got the idea for this activity from the novel *The Dice Man* (Reinhart 1971)

DREAM COUNTRIES: CREATIVE CLOZE DIALOGUES
Procedure

1 Draw a map of your ideal country on the board.
2 Explain its features.
3 Ask the learners each to draw the map of their ideal country.
4 After about five minutes, learners explain their map to a neighbour.
5 **Either:**
    a Ask the learners to describe how they would live out an ideal life in this country.
    b Then ask them to vividly describe their every action there. If they ski, make them describe the sensation and the run, if they laze in the sun, detail the smells, the sounds and the dreams (according to level).
    Or:
    Ask the learners to describe how the people of this land live out their lives, how their society is regulated, what they do.
6 Ask the learners to write a description of a typical day in their country. They must omit a verb, adjective or noun from each sentence, leaving a blank in each case.
7 Ask them to hand the description to another learner who must try to fill in the blanks.
8 Ask the learner who has completed filling in description to read it back to its original author. The author will then agree or disagree with each completion, for example:

LEARNER A Every morning you swim into this sea here.
LEARNER B I don't just swim, I dive into it.

6.4

LEVEL
Intermediate

EXTRAS
None

TIME
60 minutes

LANGUAGE FOCUS
The present simple

SKILLS FOCUS
All four

Randal Holme

HABITS
Procedure

1 Learners at individual tables arranged higgledy-piggledy around the room. Begin with two minutes of choral intoning *I will succeed! I will succeed!* .... At any stage thereafter any individual may self-abase with slogans such as *I will succeed, I will reform, I will amend*, etc.
2 Spend ten or fifteen minutes writing in our five individual habits in the spaces on the top half of the handout.
3 As each of us finishes, we find a partner, inquire about each others' habits, and attempt to counsel each other. Only when we get genuinely good advice do we write anything in below the dotted line on the handout.
4 Work with as many different partners as time allows.
5 It helps to video some of the discussions or to video interviews with members of the class aiming at discovering what's been found out – that is, ways in which people think they may change in the future, etc.

6.5

LEVEL
Lower intermediate +

EXTRAS
Video equipment

TIME
35 to 60 minutes

LANGUAGE FOCUS
The future with *will*

SKILLS FOCUS
Speaking, listening, and writing

Peter Grundy

Watching the video makes a better end to the session than having a class discussion.

NOTE

This activity enables us to work as individuals to begin with and then to work through a number of partners spending just as long with each as is useful. It's a very simple idea requiring no real preparation and it works like a dream.

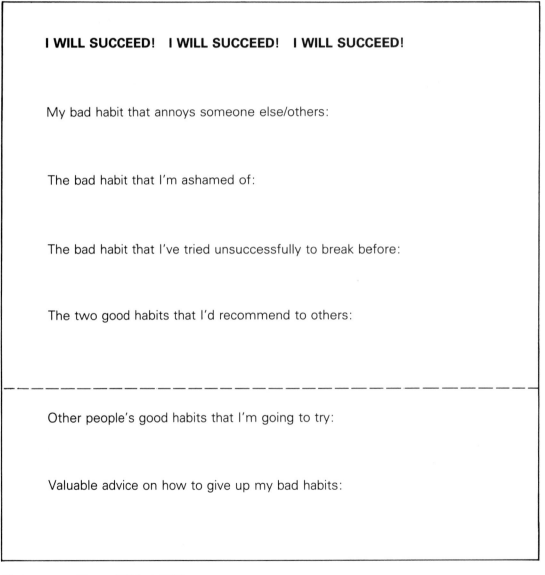

I WILL SUCCEED!   I WILL SUCCEED!   I WILL SUCCEED!

My bad habit that annoys someone else/others:

The bad habit that I'm ashamed of:

The bad habit that I've tried unsuccessfully to break before:

The two good habits that I'd recommend to others:

- -

Other people's good habits that I'm going to try:

Valuable advice on how to give up my bad habits:

LOST MEMORY SCRIPTS

Procedure

1 Speak to your class about how people rely a lot on writing things down and storing them to avoid remembering them. Sometimes mind storage is more reliable than paper or diskette.
2 Tell them a story about someone who lost all their written records and who had to recreate the content from memory. There are many such tales. For example, the Belgian historian, Henri Pirenne, wrote one of the most influential histories of Europe ever, while in internment in World War One. He had not a single book to refer to.
3 Ask each to think back to a book they read as a child or a book someone read to them as a child. Explain that maybe they will remember not something read but something told, that maybe they will recall something they imagined themselves, that they were neither read nor told.
4 Ask your learners to imagine all trace has been destroyed of whatever it is that they have recalled, apart from what they remember of it.
5 Ask everyone to describe what they remember to people round them.

6.6

LEVEL
Elementary +

EXTRAS
None

TIME
15 to 30 minutes

AIM
To generate discussion

Mario Rinvolucri

AROUND THE WORLD

Procedure

1 Pass out copies of a weather report (like Fig. 12, on page 72).
2 Ask learners to look at the weather information and to do the following tasks:
   a Put a circle round every place which is NOT the capital of its country.
   b Write down the countries these circled places are in.
   c Tick all the places that you associate with holidays or leisure.
   d List all the African towns given.
   e List all the South American towns given.
   f Write down ten major cities which are not given.
   g What principles of selection might govern the inclusion/exclusion of places in the list?
3 Learners compare answers and discuss.

RATIONALE

The above questions are not typical textbook questions. By asking your learners to process the information, you lead them into greater depth. By asking them to view the information from the position of those who assembled it, you force them to comprehend it as process and intention.

6.7

LEVEL
Elementary to intermediate

EXTRAS
An international weather report. Optional, a handout with questions

TIME
30 to 40 minutes

SKILLS FOCUS
Writing, speaking, and listening

AIM
To explore a way of thinking about information from other perspectives

John Morgan

WEATHER FORECAST
NOON: 22 JULY

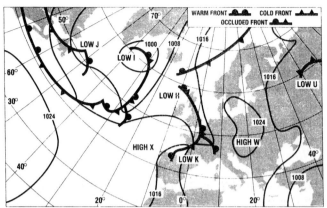

High W declining with a new centre forming further north. High X slow moving, strengthening a little. Low U moving slowly north-east Low H moving north-north-east, filling slowly. Low I slow moving, little change. Low J moving east-north-east and deepening.

WORLD WEATHER

YESTERDAY, MIDDAY:c,cloud;f,fair,fg,fog;r,rain;sn,snow;s,sunny

City	C F	City	C F	City	C F	City	C F
Aberdeen	r 14 57	Cardiff	s 29 84	Kingston*	s 31 88	Paris*	f 37 99
Aberdovey	f 29 84	Carlisle	f 25 77	Kuala Lumpur	f 32 90	Peking	r 28 82
Accra	c 27 81	Casablanca	s 31 88	Las Palmas	s 27 81	Perth	r 15 59
Ajaccio	s 28 82	Chicago	c 22 71	Lerwick	c 13 55	Plymouth	s 28 82
Akrotiri	s 29 84	Christchurch	r 5 41	Lima	c 18 64	Port Stanley*	c 3 37
Alexandria	s 28 82	Cologne	s 25 77	Lisbon	f 31 88	Prague	f 20 68
Algiers	s 33 91	Copenhagen	f 22 72	Liverpool	f 26 79	Reykjavik	r 8 46
Amsterdam	f 29 77	Corfu	s 30 86	Lizard	s 21 70	Rhodes	s 27 81
Anchorage*	r 13 55	Dakar	s 29 84	Locarno	s 27 81	Rio de Janeiro	f 27 80
Anglesey	c 25 77	Darwin	s 25 77	London	s 29 84	Riyadh*	s 44 111
Athens	f 32 90	Dover	f 25 77	Los Angeles	c 32 89	Rome	f 31 88
Auckland	c 9 48	Dublin	c 23 73	Luxembourg	s 26 79	Ronaldsway	c 19 66
Ayr	c 19 66	Dubrovnik	s 27 81	Madrid	f 37 99	Salzburg	s 25 77
Bahrain	c 41 106	Edinburgh	c 16 61	Majorca	s 31 88	San Francisco	c 24 74
Bangkok	f 33 91	Faro	f 34 93	Malaga	s 30 86	San Juan	c 33 92
Barbados	c 30 87	Florence	s 29 84	Malta	f 29 84	Santiago	c 16 61
Barcelona	f 28 82	Frankfurt	f 27 81	Manchester	c 25 77	Seoul	f 27 81
Beirut*	f 26 79	Funchal	f 26 79	Manila	r 33 91	Singapore	f 32 90
Belfast	f 20 68	Geneva*	f 26 78	Mecca	c 46 114	Southampton	s 24 75
Belgrade	f 28 82	Gibraltar	s 28 82	Melbourne	s 10 50	Southend	f 23 73
Berlin*	c 20 68	Glasgow	r 18 64	Mexico City	c 29 79	Stockholm	f 21 69
Bermuda	f 28 82	Guernsey	s 25 77	Miami	f 32 89	Stornoway	r 17 63
Berwick	c 19 66	Harare	c 16 61	Milan	s 28 82	Strasbourg	s 28 82
Biarritz	f 35 95	Havana	f 33 91	Mombasa*	f 26 79	Sydney	f 17 63
Birmingham	c 27 81	Helsinki	c 24 76	Montevideo	f 17 62	T'aipei	f 34 93
Blackpool	c 24 75	Hong Kong	f 32 90	Montreal	c 26 79	Tel Aviv	f 30 86
Bogota	c 17 63	Honolulu	c 30 86	Moscow	c 25 77	Tenerife	s 30 86
Bombay	f 30 86	Inverness	r 16 61	Munich	s 25 77	Tiree	r 17 63
Bordeaux	s 33 91	Ipswich	f 23 73	Nairobi	c 18 64	Tokyo	f 31 88
Bournemouth	s 28 82	Islamabad	f 34 93	Nassau	c 33 91	Toronto	r 21 79
Brighton	s 24 75	Isles of Scilly	s 22 72	Newcastle	c 23 73	Tunis	s 34 93
Brisbane	s 15 59	Istanbul	f 26 79	New Delhi	c 39 102	Valencia	f 33 91
Bristol	s 29 84	Jakarta	c 32 90	Newquay	s 22 72	Vancouver	c 23 73
Brussels	f 29 84	Jeddah	s 34 93	New York	r 23 73	Venice	s 26 79
Budapest	f 27 80	Jersey	f 29 84	Nice	s 26 79	Vienna	f 25 77
Buenos Aires	c 17 62	Jerusalem	f 29 84	Nicosia	f 36 97	Warsaw	r 18 64
Cairo	f 32 90	Johannesburg	f 12 54	Norwich	f 22 72	Washington*	s 28 82
Calgary	c 30 86	Karachi	c 31 88	Nottingham	f 27 81	Wellington	f 9 48
Cape Town	s 21 70	Kathmandu	c 23 73	Oslo	f 21 70	York	f 23 73
Caracas	r 26 79	Kiev	c 15 59	Oxford	c 29 84	Zurich	s 26 79

*Latest available figure

Sun rises : 5.07am		Sun sets : 9.05pm	
Moon rises : 10.34m		Moon sets : 9.50am	

Last quarter 25th July

LIGHTING UP TIMES

London	9.34pm to 4.39am
Bristol	9.44pm to 4.50am
Birmingham	9.45pm to 4.42am
Manchester	9.52pm to 4.39am
Newcastle	9.57pm to 4.28am
Glasgow	10.13pm to 4.34am
Belfast	10.13pm to 4.48am

HIGH TIDES

TODAY	AM	HT	PM	HT
London Bridge	5.09	7.3	3.19	7.1
Liverpool	2.16	9.6	2.41	9.1
Avonmouth	10.35	13.1	10.55	13.3
Hull(Albert Dock)	9.25	7.6	9.03	7.3
Greenock	3.22	3.6	3.59	3.1
Dun Laoghaire	2.23	4.3	3.01	3.8

Height measured in metres

Fig. 12
In a recent paper find a weather report like this one which lists lots of cities

POSITIVE AND NEGATIVE EFFECTS OF GOALS

Procedure

6.8

LEVEL
Intermediate +

EXTRAS
None

TIME
30 minutes

LANGUAGE FOCUS
Second conditionals

SKILLS FOCUS
Listening, writing and speaking

Rena Subotnik

1 Elicit a wish from learners, e.g. *I can play any music I like at home.*
2 Encourage learners to generate a comprehensive list of the good and bad consequences of this wish being fulfilled. Ask your learners to write their thoughts down in this format:

+ ME (THE STUDENT) −	
I would feel really happy when I was at home and feel as if I had more rights.	I wouldn't want to do any homework or housework. I'd just want to listen to music.

Orally pool some of the different things people have thought of to make sure that everyone knows what you want. Then continue, allowing time for writing at every step.

3 Ask what might be positive and negative consequences for their families if the goal were accomplished, e.g.,

+ FAMILY −	
I would feel better so I'd be better company around the house.	I wouldn't spend as much time out of my room or helping the others, so there wouldn't be much family time.

4 Ask, *If this goal were accomplished, what might be the consequences for your community?*

+ COMMUNITY −	
I would spend less time with my cassette recorder in the street, so the streets would be more peaceful.	My friends and I would stay at home more so there'd be less of the 'street life' that makes our community colourful.

5 And then ask, *If this goal were accomplished, what might be the consequences for your country?*

+ COUNTRY −	
With so much music at home more people would grow up wanting to play an instrument.	Learners would fail school exams. Discos would close. Parents and grandparents would press for THEIR music at home too.

6 Then ask, *If this goal were accomplished, what might be the positive and negative consequences for the world?*

+ WORLD −	
Relationships between different generations would be better, if everybody was allowed time to play the music they liked.	People would be unlikely to want to listen to other people's music at home. Irritation and quarrelling would increase all over the world.

7 When these steps have been completed, learners can discuss:
   a Whether it was equally easy to analyse things from both positive and negative sides, and ...
   b Whether some ideas could be thought of to alleviate some of the negative consequences and bolster the positive ones.

6.9

LEVEL
Intermediate +

EXTRAS
None

TIME
30 to 60 minutes

SKILLS FOCUS
Speaking, listening, writing

Rena Subotnik

WORKING BACKWARDS FROM GOALS

Procedure

1 Learners either as whole class (the first time) or in smaller groups (if they've done this activity before), decide on a long-term goal. The goal should be clearly stated and a date given by which they hope to have reached it. e.g., '1994   Nobody dying of hunger in Ethiopia.'
2 Orally or in writing, work backwards year by year towards the present, describing what human action could be taken to lead to the next event that in turn will lead to the final goal, e.g.,

1993 Workshops to show rural people how to plant new types of rice and trees and make best use of new irrigation systems.
1992 Transport system from west and north outside country and system from ports in the country improved. War in Eritrea ended by new President. Research into fast growing trees is finished.
1991 New wells and irrigations systems installed by Chinese workers. Research done into resistant rice that needs little water. 'Band Aid' money continues to solve immediate needs.
1990 Research is done with different types of wells and irrigation systems. Coup in Ethiopia leads to better relationships with the north of the country.

Try to steer learners away from including flukes and catastrophes. If the goal chosen is dated far in advance, then of course the intervals could be much more than one year.

3 Evaluate whole class or smaller group work by discussing:
   a Whether the process of working backwards from a goal suggested steps towards practical and creative solutions
   b Whether the choice of goal was a good one
   c What other types of goal you could choose
   d Whether the working backwards idea is a way of solving problems that could be useful in other areas of life.
4 For the next goal you might like to chose, 'Next year: being able to communicate well in English'!

CHAPTER 7

Story telling

I am convinced that no lesson is better than one in which a learner tells a good story.

DO-IT-YOURSELF STORY
Procedure

1 Give the learners a series of questions which suggest a story. The ones shown are suitable for lower to upper intermediate learners:

How long had the three astronauts been on the planet Hara?
What were they doing on the planet?
What signs of life had they seen?
Why did Kavanah leave the others and go off alone?
How far away from the spaceship did he walk?
When did he realise that something was following him?
Describe the creature that almost caught him.
While he was running away, how did he know that the creature was just behind him?
When he tripped and fell into the crater, what was he sure was going to happen?
Why did Kavanah get such a surprise?
Can you think of a good title for your story?

2 Make sure everyone understands that they are not simply to write a list of answers but that, by answering the questions, they write a story and that this should be in story form on the page.
3 Learners write individually. Ask them to sign their papers.
4 The first two learners to finish, swap and read each other's stories. As others finish they also swap stories. When people finish reading one story, they may swap for another.
5 Silent reading continues until even the last writers to finish have also had a chance to read at least one other person's story.
6 Ask people to say which story they liked best. Explain, though, that no one may nominate their own story.
7 When a story is nominated, its author reads it out loud. Two or three stories are read out in this way.

Adapted by the editor from *Do-It-Yourself Short Story Writing* in *Day by Day* Creton 1983, page 21). A different version of this activity also appears in *Recipes for Tired Teachers* (Sion 1985).

7.1

LEVEL
Elementary +

EXTRAS
Questions which suggest a story

TIME
30 to 90 minutes

SKILLS FOCUS
All four

John-Paul Creton

7.2

LEVEL
Elementary +

EXTRAS
Tape recorders

TIME
40 to 90 minutes, depending on class size

SKILLS FOCUS
Speaking

Cynthia Beresford

SOUND SEQUENCE

Procedure

Before class:

1 Individually, in pairs or in small groups – learners prepare sequences of sounds. Learners can make their sounds anyway they like. If each learner or group has a tape recorder, they can record their sound sequences. Otherwise, they may need to bring various sound making objects to class unless, that is, they propose to make all their sounds themselves.

2 Each set of sound makers prepares a written 'score' specifying which sounds come in which order and saying how the sounds were produced. This will come in handy later.

In class:

3 The sequences of sounds are played (if on tape) or made 'live'. If they are done live, it's best that the sound makers are at the back of the class, unseen by the rest of the class.

4 The 'audience', in pairs, prepare stories to fit the sound sequences. They may ask the sound makers for repetitions at any time. (For this reason, the sound makers should have notes fixing the order their sounds come in.)

You must give learners guidance as to whether the events are to be recounted as if immediate or as if in the past. In the former case naturally told stories will use the present forms – simple, continuous, and perfect. In the latter case, the simple past will predominate. The former is more natural, but more difficult.

5 When the stories are ready, they are told to the whole group, each time with the accompaniment of the sound sequence.

6 Afterwards, the sound makers explain how they made their noises and say, as well, what stories they had in mind.

ACKNOWLEDGEMENT

The idea of using sound sequences as a basis for story telling comes from *Sounds Interesting* (Maley and Duff 1975) and *Sounds Intriguing* (Maley and Duff 1978).

STORIES FROM TAPES

Procedure

1 Divide the class into two groups (ideally 4–8 learners per group).
2 Invite each group to think of a story. Let them organise themselves as they like. For example, one learner can tell an interesting story they know or the group can invent a story. The only condition is that the story is not known by the other group, so no well-known tales.
3 When the story has been told within the group, the group members think of twenty comprehension questions about the story. (Less than twenty gives a poor selection).
4 The members of each group work as a team to record their twenty questions.
5 The tapes are exchanged and the learners listen to the questions but they don't try to answer them. Instead, they make notes.
6 After they have listened to all twenty questions, they try to imagine the story of the other group.
7 In a whole class session, each group tells their 'story from questions'. Or, pair together groups who have swapped tapes. Sometimes the story told is similar to the original but very often the result is a new one.

ACKNOWLEDGEMENT

This activity is a more learner-centred version of the exercise on page 80 of *Once Upon a Time* (Morgan and Rinvolucri 1983).

7.3

LEVEL
Elementary +

EXTRAS
Cassette players and blank cassettes

TIME
30 to 40 minutes

LANGUAGE FOCUS
The simple past, also in questions

SKILLS FOCUS
Speaking, listening, and note taking

Christine Frank

BEHIND A SONG

Procedure

1 The learners find or transcribe the lyrics from a song they like or you furnish them with the lyrics of a suitable song. Each learner needs different lyrics.
2 The learners read the lyrics and prepare to tell a story based on them. You will probably need to help them with difficult language.

In class:
3 Each learner tells their story. This can be done before the whole class, if numbers are not large, or in groups.
4 The listeners try to guess the title of the song.
5 Next, each learner visually presents the lyrics to their song. This can be done on handouts (photocopied in advance), on posters, or on OHP transparencies. Each learner explains any difficult language to the others.

VARIATION

The songs may be in the learners' mother tongue(s).

7.4

LEVEL
Intermediate +

EXTRAS
Each student needs the lyrics of a different song

TIME
Very dependent on class size

SKILLS FOCUS
Reading, speaking, and listening

Jim Wingate

7.5

LEVEL
Elementary

EXTRAS
None

TIME
60 to 70 minutes

SKILLS FOCUS
Listening and
speaking

Judith Baker

SEVEN STAGES STORY TELLING

Find one good story and learn it well enough to be able to tell it from memory, without changing it, more than seven times. The effect isn't the same if you read it. In any case, you'd be using a crutch that you will be asking your learners to do without.

The story must have more than one character in it. It's best if the story has reported rather than direct speech in it, although reported speech itself is not strictly necessary.

Procedure

1 Tell your story to the class.
2 Put your class into groups so that the number of people in each group is the same as the number of characters in the story.
3 The learners, in their groups, decide who is which character. (In the cases of discrepant numbers, some learners can have two roles.)
4 Explain to the learners that you are going to tell the story again, and that as you do everyone must mime the actions made by their character in the story. Then tell the story.
5 Now, explain that everyone must make noises appropriate to their character and tell the story a third time.
6 Tell the story, but pause frequently. Learners must add the missing words.
7 Tell the story a fifth time, but leave a gap everywhere dialogue can be inserted. Learners insert it.
8 Tell the story again, with more pauses and gaps to be filled. Elicit the missing bits.
9 Ask learners to perform the story with dialogue and action. One group member may provide linking commentary. Ask them to change part of the story, perhaps the ending. Give them time to rehearse.
10 While they are rehearsing, tell the whole story again and again. They may seem not to be listening but they are.
11 The stories are acted out, before the whole class or before other groups.

STORIES FROM THINGS

Collect enough objects to be able to give twenty to every pair in class, e.g. buttons (very cheap from second hand shops and grannies), playing cards, photos, chessmen, foreign coins, stamps, small bottles, twigs, feathers, fishing lures ... anything except things normally found in classrooms.

Procedure

1 Gather the class around you so they can all see the objects when you place them on a table.
2 Tell a story from your own life using some of the objects you have brought with you. Look at the objects as you tell the story, not at the learners. Use the objects to represent characters or events or individual words (e.g. a feather can stand for *flew*). After introducing the objects, place them in some meaningful order on the table.
3 At the end of your story, allow questions but when you answer them, focus on the relevant objects (e.g. pick them up, look at them ...) not on the questioner. Perhaps you can indicate an answer by using certain objects as signs which you may point to in a meaningful order. For example, pointing to an object which represents a person in your story, then pointing to the feather, and then pointing to the object representing a certain place can mean, X flew to Y.
4 When there are no further questions, give twenty objects to each learner, or allow everyone to choose for themself.
5 The learners tell each other stories in pairs or small groups, using the objects as props as in your demonstration.
6 If you want the learners to practise a particular word or grammatical element, you can try this; Give each learner, in addition to their other objects, several small white buttons. Tell them each button means *had to* and that they must use all their white buttons in telling their story.

7.6

LEVEL
Intermediate +

EXTRAS
Lots of objects

TIME
45 to 90 minutes

SKILLS FOCUS
Listening and speaking

Cynthia Beresford

7.7

A STORY FROM CLUES

LEVEL

Upper elementary +

EXTRAS

None

TIME

1st lesson, 10 minutes; 2nd lesson, 2 minutes; 3rd lesson, 30 to 40 minutes

LANGUAGE FOCUS

The Simple Past; contrastive stress

SKILLS

All four

Tessa Woodward

A STORY FROM CLUES

Procedure

FIRST LESSON:

1 Explain to your learners that they must keep a record for one whole day of all the things they read. Ask them to make a note of the times that they read these things too. This is for homework. You should get lists that look something like this:

TIME	WHAT I READ
7.05	clock face
7.15	toothpaste tube
7.30	side of Royal Mail van
7.35	road atlas
7.45–8.00	traffic signs ... numbers on gear stick
8.05	watch face
8.07	parking meter instructions
8.15	cash dispenser instructions

and so on. Learners may well need help with individual vocabulary items.

SECOND LESSON:

2 Take the lists in.

BEFORE THE THIRD LESSON:

3 Re-write or re-type the lists so that the original handwriting is changed. Omit learners' names. Number the new sheets.

THIRD LESSON:

4 Give out copies of the lists so that no learner has their own list.
5 Ask learners to discuss each entry and its implications (e.g. *why would you read the gear lever numbers if it was your own car?*).
6 Then they compose either an oral or written account of the day they've read about. It can be as dramatic or bland as they like.
7 The stories are told or circulated.
8 People guess whose day it was. The original person can say how near or far the story is from reality. (This is good for practise of contrastive stress, e.g. *Well, actually I didn't drive to London; I drove to SouthHAMPton.*).

PATTERN STORIES AND VERB/NOUN MATCHING

Stories that repeat themselves according to a pre-set pattern were a traditional way for the story teller to invite audience participation, they are also a useful way for you to get learners to do your work as well as theirs, thus enhancing their language practice. After a while the learners can carry the story forward with little more than a few cues from you. These can even be 'inserted' with mime. The following story of Lazy Jack is an example:

In a far away country and long ago, there lived a sad princess. She never smiled or laughed and her parents worried about her.

In the same country there lived a young man called Lazy Jack. Jack lived with his mother and never did any work. He just watched while she did everything.

One day, Jack's mother got fed up and told Jack to go out to work.

The next day Jack went to work for a carpenter. He spent a day working with wood and tidying the shop. The carpenter was pleased and gave him a coin at the end of the day. Jack put the coin in his trouser pocket and went home. On the way home, he jumped over a river and the coin fell out of his pocket.

When Jack got home his mother asked him what the carpenter had given him. Jack looked in his pocket and could not find the coin. His mother got angry and said, 'Next time, put it in your jacket pocket.'

The next day, Jack went to work at a dairy. The dairy owner was pleased and gave him a jug of milk. Jack remembered what his mother said and poured the milk in his jacket pocket. When he got home, his mother asked him what the owner of the dairy had given him and Jack only showed her a wet pocket. She said, 'Next time, carry it home in your arms'.

The next day, Jack went to work in a sausage factory. The factory owner was pleased and gave Jack a cat. Jack remembered what his mother said and carried it home in his arms but the cat scratched him and ran away. Jack's mother was angry and said, 'Next time bring it home on a string'.

The next day, Jack went to work in a bakers. The baker was pleased and gave Jack a large cake. Jack remembered what his mother said and took it home on a string. When he reached home, he had no cake. His mother was very angry and said, 'Next time, bring it home on your head'.

The next day, Jack went to work in a cheese factory. The owner was pleased and gave him a big cheese. Jack remembered what his mother said and carried it home on his head. The sun was hot and melted the cheese. His mother was very angry and said, 'Next time, carry it home on your back'.

The next day, Jack went to work in a stable. The owner was pleased and gave him donkey to take home. Jack remembered what his mother said and carried it home on his back. The sad princess was looking out of her window and when she saw a man carrying a donkey she had to

7.8

LEVEL
Elementary to intermediate

EXTRAS
One pattern story

TIME
90 minutes

LANGUAGE FOCUS
Simple past, vocabulary

SKILLS
All four

Randal Holme

smile, then she laughed and laughed. Her parents were so pleased that they asked Jack to marry her and Jack never had to work again in his life.

Procedure

1 Tell this story and ask the learners to embellish it by telling you the details of his jobs, etc., and as soon as they get the pattern ask them to tell you what comes next, giving only such cues as *the owner gave him a cat*, or *the cat scratched him*.
2 When the story is finished, divide the learners into two groups. Ask one group to tell the story to another and to write down all the important verbs in a list. Ask the other group to do the same by writing down all the important nouns.
3 Pair off noun learners with verb learners and ask them to make sentences about the story by matching nouns and verbs. Thus a noun learner may have written 'princess' and a verb learner 'laughed'. They may then produce a sentence like, *The princess never laughed.*

   The exercise could be made more complicated with an additional adjective/adverb group who not only listed the adjectives/adverbs they remembered but added their own as an embellishment.
4 The matched words can be used as a core for a written version of the story.

CHAPTER 8

Especially writing

The following activities all aim to foster fluency in writing. Other skills are always involved, but writing is the thing. In every case, the aim is for learners to write for an audience, not for attraction of your red ink.

HYPOTAXIA

Procedure

1 Hand out copies of the text and have everyone read the text a couple of times, as it is short, and show they are finished by turning the text over.
2 Ask everyone to form pairs and make a list of vocabulary items from the text without referring to it.
3 When the lists are looking healthy, ask everyone, still in pairs, to write a sentence, just one sentence, using items from their lists and which is as unrelated to the original text as possible.
   There is no need for anyone to refer to the text. New vocabulary certainly can be brought in to the composition.
4 Ask everyone to read their sentences aloud if they would like to, and so demonstrate how unrelated all their unrelated sentences can be.

RATIONALE

This is a good mental preparation for longer writing tasks where you wish people to express themselves as individually as possible but feel that your learners are too used to all producing the same sort of work, perhaps because they have come through a very traditional educational system with a great emphasis on conformity.

8.1

LEVEL
Intermediate +

EXTRAS
A short text

TIME
10 to 25 minutes

SKILLS FOCUS
All four

AIM
To practise writing long sentences creatively

Rick Cooper

8.2

LEVEL

Elementary +

EXTRAS

Pens and lots of slips
of paper

TIME

20 to 60 minutes per
session

SKILLS FOCUS

Writing and reading

AIM

Communicating in
writing

Mario Rinvolucri

LETTER WRITING: THE INITIAL IDEA

Procedure

1 Give each learner several small pieces of paper or ask them to tear or cut sheets of notepaper into quarters or sixths.
2 Explain that everyone is going to write letters to other people in the group. Each letter must be addressed, signed and then delivered as soon as it has been written.
3 The learners write and deliver answers to the letters they have received. Join in the exercise as a full participant.

I learnt this exercise from Kris Markowski in Paris. I later heard that the same exercise is used to allow reflective one-to-one communication towards the end of a therapy week or week-end.

VARIATIONS

a i After the writing stage learners negotiate with each other which letters are to be pooled for correction and which should remain private to their writers and addressees.

  ii The 'public' letters are then stuck up round the walls and communally corrected. Of course, at the same time learners have some interesting, personal reading to do.

b A colleague in German adult education was worried about marginal members of her group when she heard the initial idea. She was maternally concerned about learners no one would want to write to. Her modification is:

  i Ask each learner to write a signed letter without addressee.

  ii People place their letters on a central table.

  iii Each learner takes one and answers it.

  In this way everybody gets a letter to set them going.

c When I presented Markowski's initial idea to a group of Belgians who teach languages to the unemployed, some leapt up and transformed the exercise into written role play, that is:

  i Learners take on business roles.

  ii They write each other letters (e.g. letters of complaint) in role.

LETTER WRITING: CYNTHIA'S VARIATION
Procedure

1 Start the idea by setting ten minutes for each learner to write one letter to you and deliver it personally.
2 Meanwhile, you write letters to three or four learners and deliver them.
3 After class, answer each learner's letter without correcting or commenting on their use of language, but genuinely answering the letters as real communication.
4 Next day deliver your replies and invite the learners to write to anyone in the group, not just you.
5 During this writing time write to more learners and deliver the letters. Some teachers at this point write letters to learners they fear no one else may write to.
6 Gradually the onus of reading and writing moves from the teacher to the learners.

8.3

LEVEL
Elementary +

EXTRAS
Small slips of paper

TIME
Two sessions, fifteen minutes for the first, longer for the second

SKILLS FOCUS
Reading and writing

PREPARATION
Reply to learners' letters

Cynthia Beresford

SECRET CORRECTION

In my own mind the most effective correction techniques are those in which the person corrected is unconscious of being corrected. All teacherly correction has a paternal or maternal tinge to it, and for some learners, particularly adolescents, this is negative. Among adult learners I have often noticed that the people who most clamour for heavy teacher correction are those least able to internalise it and make it part of their unconscious learning styles.

But what about 'secret' correction? A good example is when the teacher writes letters to his or her learners

8.4

LEVEL
Beginner +

EXTRAS
None

TIME
As long as necessary

Mario Rinvolucri

Procedure

1 Write a letter to 'Dear Everybody' and each learner who wants to replies.
2 Reply to each letter individually. It's a lot of work, but rewarding and interesting. Do not return the learners' letters to them. To do so would wreck the correspondences. It is your letters of reply that offer the learners models.
3 Very often the learner 'steals' grammar, phrases and words from your letter in replying to it. When a Greek learner of mine wrote about the '1922 Micro-Asiatic Expedition', I naturally referred in my reply to the '1922 Asia Minor Campaign'. This was secret correction in the sense that the learner was reading my letter for content and yet was picking

up the correct form of the phrase she had got wrong. If she was one of those people who dislikes being corrected, in this instance there is a good chance that her defences were circumvented.

8.5

LEVEL
Post-beginner +

EXTRAS
None

TIME
30 to 40 minutes

SKILLS FOCUS
Speaking, listening and writing

Mario Rinvolucri

I HAVE A SCRIBE

This is an absorbing and demanding exercise which involves a great deal of spoken and written negotiation.

Procedure

1 Ask the learners to pair off with someone they get on with.
2 Tell them they are going to write short letters to other people in the group. If learner A in a pair wants to write a letter to X across the room, A tells their partner, B, what to write. A does not write the letter, B does. Learner B, A's scribe, delivers the finished letter to X. X can only reply by dictating a letter to their partner, Y.
3 Wind the exercise up before people drop off in their chairs from excited exhaustion!

ACKNOWLEDGEMENT

This idea came up during a brainstorm on dictation at INFOP in Dijon, France. It arises from thinking of village letter writing in preliterate cultures.

THEME LETTERS

Letter writing in class round a theme can open up subsequent discussion.

Procedure

1 Propose the theme and ask the learners to write letters to each other on this theme.
2 Explain that as soon as a learner has written and signed a letter to another person in the group they deliver it and that the other person may answer it or not.
3 After twenty to thirty minutes' writing, each person who has a letter they would like to make public goes and asks the writer of the letter if making it public is OK.
4 Learners then read the letters out round the group. Animated discussion will often grow out of this.

VARIATION

I have used the technique in teacher training situations too. I had to give a seminar on 'getting the learners to plan their own course'. To help teachers explore their feelings about this proposal we did the above letter writing exercise. This allowed several colleagues to state quite clearly that they felt uneasy about searching for ways of handing over planning power to learners.

RATIONALE

The addressee-focused writing phase allows people to marshall and clarify their own thoughts before being over-influenced by others in the discussion. The writing frustrates some learners and makes them more eager to speak, while protecting those who need more time to express themselves.

8.6

LEVEL
Lower
intermediate +

EXTRAS
None

TIME
40 to 60 minutes

SKILLS FOCUS
All four

AIM
To prepare for a
discussion

Mario Rinvolucri

8.7

LEVEL
Elementary +

EXTRAS
A poem

TIME
Twenty to thirty
minutes per variation

SKILLS FOCUS
All four

Paul Fagg

OPEN THE DOOR

Procedure

1 Before reading the poem, lead a warm up with a relaxation and dream
journey. You say, for example:

Relax. Sit comfortably. Feel your fingers loose and relaxed, now
your arms warm and heavy, your shoulders soft, your neck relaxed
and comfortable. Feel your face relaxing, all tension going out of your
forehead, your eyebrows, feel your lips and tongue relaxed and close
your eyes. Now feel your breathing easy and rhythmic in . . . out . . . in
. . . out . . . and the relaxation going down your stomach to your legs,
even your feet and toes are relaxed, and the warmth and softness
coming up your legs to relax your back. Now you are completely
relaxed, I'm going to take you on a short journey. You are in a room.
In your imagination look around the room. See what is in the room
. . . see what is on the walls. Look at the ceiling . . . and the floor . . .
Feel where you are sitting or standing or lying in the room . . . Feel
the contact of your clothes on your skin and feel the weight and
balance of how you are sitting or standing or lying . . . Feel the warmth
or cold, dampness or dryness of the room on your skin . . . Breathe in
. . . what are the smells of the room . . . listen . . . to the sounds you
can hear in the room . . . walk around the room and reach out and
touch things in the room . . . feel the things, cool or warm, heavy or
light, rough or smooth, soft or hard . . . Now you know the room
completely, you see a door. It is closed . . . listen

2 Read the poem aloud.
3 After the poem, ask learners to turn to a neighbour and just talk about
the room they visualised and the poem, give them about two minutes.
4 Then read the poem aloud again.

VARIATIONS

a Immediately after the visualisation . . .
   i Ask learners to tell a partner what's on the other side of their
   door. Give them one minute to talk.
   ii Then ask each learner to write a description of what is on the
   other side of the door and to express how they feel about it. Give
   them five to ten minutes.
   iii As soon as each is finished writing, encourage them to go and
   read what they have written to someone else who has finished
   writing too.
b Instead of writing, learners can draw their room and what is outside.

CHAPTER 9

One-to-one

Much one-to-one teaching is to business people. Unfortunately, many teachers involved in one-to-one teaching of business people have the mistaken idea that business people invariably prefer staid and unimaginative teaching. If you can explain why a particular activity is likely to help them learn – that is, 'sell' the activity — business people are *at least* as adventurous as any learners.

ONE-TO-ONE PERSONALISED LISTENING COMPREHENSION

Procedure

1 Ask a learner to come to class prepared to give a five minute talk/presentation/sales pitch or whatever in their mother tongue.
2 The learner gives their talk, breaking it up into one or two sentence chunks, so that you can consecutively interpret into English. If the leaner thinks they have been mis-interpreted, a re-statement in the mother tongue is in order.
3 Record the whole process.
4 The learner goes through the bi-lingual tape listening hard to the English 'they' have magically produced, noting down things they are unsure of, new words, etc ... They may pick out further mis-interpretations. While the learner does this work the teacher is having coffee next door.
5 The learner and teacher get together again and go through any points that have struck the learner.

RATIONALE

Most listening comprehension exercises are 'third person ones'. The learners listen to people they cannot talk to who are involved with each other. If you tell your learners a story, then they are involved in 'second person' listening. They can stop you and ask a question or offer a comment. In the above exercise they are doing 'first person' listening. They are actually monitoring a foreign language version of themself going out to the world. This is possibly the most ego-involving sort of listening a person can experience.

NOTE ON INTERPRETING

You will find it easier to interpret if you sit next to your learner and a bit behind them. Unobtrusively take up the same body posture as the learner.

9.1

LEVEL
Low intermediate

EXTRAS
Tape recorder, blank cassette

TIME
45 minutes

REQUIREMENT
Teacher must understand the learners' mother tongue very well

SKILLS FOCUS
Speaking and listening

Mario Rinvolucri

As you translate, try to do it within their feeling, universe and dialect. The more you succeed in doing this, the more effective their listening comprehension will be. You have to try and give them an acceptable 'self' in English, though a self they are still linguistically quite unable to produce on their own.

ACKNOWLEDGEMENT

Bernard Dufeu's work on doubling in language teaching lies behind this exercise, as does Charles Curran's work.

This exercise came to me powerfully when I had to do a day's seminar at the Stiftung für Internationale Entwicklung – I spoke English and there was consecutive interpretation into German. I have never done more motivated or speedy listening comprehension in my life. Gradually my interpreter got better and better as he began to identify with me more and more deeply. The work entirely changed our rapport which had started off rather poorly.

9.2

LEVEL
Elementary +

EXTRAS
Typewriter and paper

TIME
20 minutes upwards

SKILLS FOCUS
Speaking and reading

Mario Rinvolucri

A WAY OUT OF A ONE-TO-ONE TEACHING SITUATION

The tête à tête can become too much. Both the learner and the teacher need some respite. One way out of the horns-locked encounter is for the learner to be given something to do on their own. Another and more interesting way is for the teacher to accomplish a task on their own, in the presence of the learner. The activity proposed below involves precisely this.

Procedure

1 For homework, ask your learner to prepare a talk on some gripping aspect of their work, looked at from an unexpected angle. If the learner is a surgeon, invite them to talk about their feelings and reactions on making the initial incision and the subsequent penetration of the patient's body.
2 The next day tell the learner you are going to type out an anticipation of their talk. In the ten minutes it takes you to do this, the learner is given nothing official to do. They may not look at what you are writing.
3 They give the prepared talk, and this is followed by questions, discussion and maybe language clean-up work.
4 The learner then reads what you wrote before listening to their talk. This may well produce further discussion.

RATIONALE

The ten minute latency period offered to the learner above allows them to mentally modify what they are going to say during the talk, to tailor it to the addressee and to go over the language to be used. During the ten minutes the learner is in one sense alone and in another in very strong contact with you.

ACKNOWLEDGEMENT

The exercise is a variation on one proposed in *Vocabulary* (Morgan 1986).

Bibliography

Bandler, R and Grinder, R 1974   *Frogs into Princes* Real People Press

Van den Bos, J 1983   Articles in *Practical English Teaching*, March

Burniston, C 1972   *Into the Life of Things: An Exploration of Language Through Verbal Dynamics* English Speaking Board

Creton, J-P   1983 *Day by Day* Pilgrims Publications

Deller, S   1990 *Lessons from the Learner* Longman

Hill, D   1990 *Visual Impact* Longman

Johnstone, K   1981 *Impro* Methuen

Maley, A and Duff, A   1975 *Sounds Interesting* CUP

Maley, A and Duff, A   1978 *Sounds Intriguing* CUP

Maley, A and Duff, A   1982 *Drama Techniques in Language Learning* CUP

McArthur, T 1981   *Longman Lexicon of Contemporary English* Longman

Morgan, J   1986 *Vocabulary* OUP

Morgan, J and Rinvolucri, M   1983 *Once Upon a Time* CUP

Postman, N and Weingartner, C 1977   *The Art of Subversive Teaching: Teaching as a Subversive Activity* Pitman

Reinhart, L 1971   *The Dice Man* Grafton Books

Sion, C 1985   *Recipes for Tired Teachers* Addision-Wesley

Underhill, A 1980   *Use Your Dictionary* OUP

Wicke, R 1988   *Storytelling im Englischunterricht* Hessiche Institut für Lehrfortbildung

Willis, J and D 1989   *Collins Cobuild English Course* Collins

Woodward, T 1988   Splitting the Atom *English Teaching Forum* (**26**) 4

Woodward, T 1990   *Models and Metaphors in Language Teacher Training* CUP